HOW TO GET YOUR FIRST COPYWRITING JOB IN ADVERTISING

711355   21.50

HOW TO GET YOUR FIRST COPYWRITING JOB IN ADVERTISING

Dick Wasserman

E. P. DUTTON / NEW YORK

This paperback edition of *How to Get Your First Copywriting Job in Advertising* first published in 1987 by E. P. Dutton

Reprinted by arrangement with Center for Advancement of Advertising

Published in the United States by E. P. Dutton,
a division of New American Library,
2 Park Avenue, New York, N.Y. 10016.

Published simultaneously in Canada by
Fitzhenry & Whiteside Limited, Toronto.

Library of Congress Catalog Card Number: 86-72833

ISBN: 0-525-48281-4

W

Designed by Stu Rosenwasser

10 9 8 7 6 5 4 3 2 1

For Barbara and Carrie

ACKNOWLEDGMENT

I want to give special thanks to my creative partner, Stu Rosenwasser. Stu, VP, Associate Creative Director at Needham Harper Worldwide in New York, is one of the ad industry's best (and best-natured) art directors. He has taught admaking at The School of Visual Arts for nearly fifteen years. As co-founder of the center for Advancement of Advertising, Stu has worked tirelessly and quite closely with me on this book. The beneficial results of his counsel, wit and wisdom are apparent on every page.

TABLE OF CONTENTS

Contents

CHAPTER 1

SHOULD YOU BE READING THIS BOOK?

A famous national magazine is in trouble. Ad pages are down. The publisher has upgraded the editorial material, but not enough people know it. The campaign your agency has recommended is not working. The agency is in danger of losing the five million dollar account. The creative director turns to you and your art director partner. "You have less than a week to come up with a campaign that'll save the account," he says. "Go to it, and show me three or four ways to go by Wednesday."

A manufacturer of soft-sided luggage wants to create a high-fashion image for his product. The agency has come up with a commercial only one director can be trusted to shoot. She works out of Paris and has a reputation as a hothead. The agency plans to send you to Paris for two weeks to scout, cast and shoot with her. They're confident you will know how to get the best out of her.

This is the world of the advertising copywriter. Fast-paced, high pressured, highly paid. A world where confident, talented, aggressive people earn very comfortable salaries and have a ball doing it. No matter how things are going, you can always be sure of one thing—you'll never be bored. A bit anxious perhaps from time to time. But never bored.

If you can write a decent letter, you can write advertising. Maybe not great advertising, but advertising that sells, advertising that's fun to pro-

1

duce, advertising that can assure you of an exciting working life in a stimulating environment. You also need some other talents, of course. The ability to get along with all sorts of highly strung, temperamental people. The ability to sell yourself and your work. A sense of timing. Tact, diplomacy, discretion, ambition. And last, but by no means least, a great deal of plain ordinary common sense.

Let's presume you're about to graduate from a prestigious art college or you're an art major at a liberal arts college and you think you'd like to become an art director in an advertising agency. Or you're a liberal arts major about to graduate with a B.A., or you have your M.A., you've been teaching high school English for two years and you're bored with it. You've done some writing on your own and you think you might like to work as an advertising copywriter. Or you're a high school or college graduate, you've tried a couple of different jobs since you left school, you think you have more to offer than those jobs have demanded and you think a job in advertising, possibly in the creative area, might be right for you.

In any event, you have no formal advertising training either as an art director or a copywriter, and you haven't the foggiest notion of how to put together an advertisement. Some of the commercials you've seen on tv seem pretty clever and lots more seem simple-minded and stupid, or just plain dull. You wonder how advertisers get away with such stuff, whether a large part of the audience really falls for it, and whether people are really paid a lot of money to dream it up. You're sure you could devise much better stuff if somebody would just explain a few of the fundamentals to you. Possibly, you've read some popular advertising books trying to learn enough about ad making to get a job in an agency, but they haven't told you very much that's useful. Maybe you've taken some college copywriting courses, but they haven't helped much either.

The best way to learn to write ads is to get on the job training in an ad agency. To get a job as a junior art director or writer, you need a portfolio. One of the main goals of this book is to help you put together a portfolio that will help get you a job.

To my knowledge, there are no books available to college students and high school graduates that explain in simple, step-by-step terms exactly what an ad is and how to go about thinking up ads good enough to land them a job in an agency.

Before you start trying to get a job as an advertising copywriter, I should make one thing clear: if, as you get into it, you don't find writing ads great fun, if coming up with headlines and visuals and copy for various products and services isn't absolutely fascinating to you, if it doesn't make time fly, forget it—copywriting is not for you. Copywriters, like other professionals, face many frustrations. Often, they work against the clock, under tight deadlines. So it's important that you love the work—the actual process of dreaming up ads and radio and tv commercials. If you get a big kick out of that, then, as the Rabbi Hillel wrote, "all the rest is commentary."

The first thing you should do is begin tearing out newspaper and magazine ads you either hate or love. Make two piles.

Get hold of a couple of the yearly annuals of *The One Show* book (American Showcase, Inc., 724 Fifth Ave, 10th floor, New York, NY 10019 (212) 245-0981.) Published in association with The One Club for Art and Copy, Inc., 251 E. 50th St., New York, NY 10022. U.S. book distribution handled by Robert Silver Associates, 95 Madison Ave., New York, NY 10016 (212-686-5630.) Study the finalists and winning entries. This book can serve, more or less, as your primary reference guide to what good ads are all about. The more annuals you can collect and study, the better off you'll be, and the faster you're likely to learn to create good ads.

Try to get a feel for how the leadlines, layouts and copy in good ads fit together and build upon each other. See if you can begin to understand what makes these ads especially provocative and persuasive.

Subscribe to *Advertising Age* and *Adweek,* or if you want to save money, read them each week in your college library. They will give you some sense of what the advertising business is all about.

If you can afford it, buy a VCR and study the commercials over and over again. Try to see how they're similar to and different from print and radio ads. Try to figure out why you like some and hate others. Try to create your own commercials. If you don't draw well, explain your visual verbally. I'll explain more about how to overcome your inability to draw later.

3

Study the rest of this book carefully. Read about how to write good ads over and over again, and practice writing ads for all sorts of products . . . hard goods (appliances, cars, razors, etc.), soft goods (sheets, clothing, etc.), packaged goods (drugstore and supermarket items) and services (banks, baseball teams, corporate ads, etc.).

The best place I know of for beginners to practice the craft is The School of Visual Arts, 209 E. 23 Street, New York, NY. Their evening copywriting courses in particular are excellent. They're taught by working professionals, all of whom have worked at top New York agencies.

Put together a portfolio of your work. If you can, get a part-time job selling. Nothing will help you learn to deal with people better than selling face to face.

How big must your portfolio be? More about that later. But briefly: any 17×22 inch vinyl carrying case with clear plastic sleeves, into which you can slide your ads, headline and layout on the left and copy on the right, will do. Most art supply stores carry such cases. I suggest you create three campaigns consisting of three ads and copy for each (nine ads in total, advertising three different products or services) and another nine or ten single ads, with copy, for each of another nine or ten products or services.

Contact local advertising agencies in your area by correspondence. Mention that you realize their time is valuable, thank them for reading your letter, and tell them how much you'd appreciate their taking a few minutes to help you out. The tone of your letter should be diplomatic, sympathetic, respectful and ambitious.

Tell the people you contact that you'd like to be a copywriter and that you've put together a speculative portfolio of your work, and would greatly appreciate constructive comments from a senior member of the staff. Ask if you can call on such and such a date for an appointment, and pick a date a week or ten days away. Your local phone book will list the agencies in your area. Unless you live in or near a very large city most of the agencies will be small.

During summers between semesters or after school, try to get a job in an agency. Working in any agency can teach you a great deal, even if you don't write any ads. While you work, try to get as deeply involved with advertising as you can. Read all the books about it you can find. Keep updating your portfolio. Keep trying to find responsible, skilled people who can give you helpful advice. If you live in or near small towns, plan to spend some time visiting ad agencies in the nearest large cities. Keep pushing to develop and improve your portfolio—it's the key to getting a job that will launch your career.

Make every effort to land a job in the summer between your junior and senior years in as large an ad agency, in as large a city as you can find. If you can't get a copywriting job, any agency job is better than no job. During your senior year, pick out the city you'd most like to live in. Study the list of agencies in that city in the Red Book or the telephone book. Learn all you can about the listed agencies. Start writing them letters early in your senior year asking for an appointment in the spring of your senior year. Try to make sure you're thoroughly familiar with each agency's work before you have your interview. The more you know about them, the brighter, more ambitious and more aggressive you will appear.

If you spend all the time I've suggested during your summer junior and senior years working on your portfolio and contacting agencies and planning your letters and trips carefully, you won't necessarily walk off the campus and into a decent job. But you'll be far ahead of all the other college graduates who have some vague idea they'd like to be copywriters but have no specific plan in mind, except to keep asking a lot of strangers for help.

Advertising people are bright, aggressive, ambitious people. They like to make and spend money and they like to have a good time doing it. They're able to put up with a lot of frustrations on the job because they enjoy their work and they enjoy living well. They'll instinctively admire a go-getter, a self starter who has thoroughly prepared him or herself for an assault on the copywriting job market.

Another advantage of all the hard work I'm suggesting, and not a small advantage, is that, after a year and a half spent writing hundreds of ads for all sorts of products, writing letters, phoning for interviews and meeting strangers and asking for their help, you may decide advertising's just not for you.

The process may prove too exhausting. You may become discouraged at the slow rate at which you seem to be learning to write ads. Each person you see may tell you different ads are good or bad, which may demoralize you. You may decide business school is more to your liking, or selling shoes or being a pilot or fighting fires. Maybe you'll enlist in the Air Force.

Fine. You will have learned early on, before you have wasted ten years writing ads, that advertising is the last way in the world you would choose to make a living. So be it. You'll have lost nothing but a little time and wasted a little energy. When you're young, you have plenty of both.

Archibald MacLeish has spoken of the important difference between the *knowledge* of the fact and the *feel* of the fact. Advertising professionals deal mostly with the *feel* of the fact.

Learning to write good ads, these professionals will tell you, involves "getting the hang of it", or "having a feel for it". The trouble is, one can't communicate "hangs" and "feels" to readers of a book. So the unfortunate truth is that there are limitations to what you can get out of any "how-to" book about copywriting, including my book. What such a book can do for you is give you a start, an initial push in the right direction. The rest depends upon your own drive and initiative.

Ads are not "written" anymore. They are *created* or *made* in most cases, by two people, writer and art director, working together. Ad making has become too sophisticated and complicated a process for one person to master completely. Today, art directors suggest headlines, campaign themes, product names and new product ideas, edit copy and participate in the "writing" of copy, while "writers" think in terms of pictures, graphic treatments, camera angles and the like, especially when it comes to television commercials. In other words, modern advertising professionals think of themselves not as "writers" and "art directors" but as "ad makers". Prospective art directors must learn to think like writers, directors, producers and salespeople, just as writers must learn to think like art directors, producers, directors and marketing people. Ultimately, the two must learn to work together.

There are some 4,000 shops in the United States which are listed as "advertising agencies" in local phone books. Many are two or three people operations whose main function is to place local supermarket, department store and movie advertising.

For convenience, I use the term "writer" to mean the *creator* of an ad, whether he or she is an art director or writer. To get a job in an agency, a junior art director needs a certain amount of technical skill and training in the production of mechanicals, type selection and the like. A writer need only know how to type, and some can't even do that. But when working as a team, both actually "write". The art director may suggest a headline, the writer the picture. More often than not, the idea or "concept" behind the ad may occur to both at the same time. So while writers rarely have much to do with type selection, photography and so on, and art directors usually edit rather than write copy, both "write" the ad in the sense that I use the word.

Beginners cannot make much progress until they cease thinking of themselves as art directors mainly interested in pictures or writers mainly interested in words, but rather as advertising people mainly interested in selling things to people through the medium of printed advertisements or filmed commercials.

The problem for most inexperienced people trying to learn to create ads is that they don't know the fundamentals. That's particularly unfortunate because the fundamentals of ad making can be taught in a few minutes.

What *does* take time is learning to apply those fundamentals so as to create fresh, innovative, interesting, effective advertisements which will appeal to what by now must be the most jaded audience in history—the American consuming public. The energy, initiative, enthusiasm, drive and determination you bring to ad making is as important as what I can teach you. Your own particular and peculiar vision of life and the world around you and your own aggressiveness will help you make your way into and possibly upward in the ad business. What I can teach you in my way, some other instructor can probably teach you just as effectively in some other way. What you personally have to offer and how hard you personally are willing to work to develop your skill and ability will, in the long run, determine how far you go in the advertising business.

More, perhaps than any other occupation, advertising reflects and is an integral part of the changing patterns of the culture around it. It changes, with the culture, at a very rapid rate. So it follows that if you are going to create successful advertising, you have to know all you can about what's going on in the world—what books are being written, what movies filmed, what tv programs are popular, what your local newspaper, *The New York Times, Time* and *Newsweek* are saying, what *For-*

tune, Forbes and *The Wall Street Journal* are in to, what the middle class and blue collar classes are thinking and worrying about, what's going on in Washington, D.C., and so on.

That means you must keep your eyes and ears open. The best ad writers are those who are interested in and intensely curious about the world around them and the people in it. That's one of the things that makes them "creative" in the first place. They are mentally lively, easily stimulated, well-informed, opinionated, well educated in the best sense of the word. I don't necessarily mean they graduated from prestigious universities, or went to college at all for that matter, or that they have advanced degrees or were English or Philosophy or Journalism majors. Nor are they necessarily "deep" or thoughtful people.

Many of the really good adpeople I know began their adult life with a burning ambition to excel at something other than advertising—gag writing, novel writing, filmmaking, comedy writing, teaching, law—but decided on advertising because they found it more interesting and in most cases, better paying.

Ad makers are usually but by no means always "readers". One of the best art directors I know almost never reads the morning newspaper and rarely picks up a book. He's a "scanner", constantly and rather casually obtaining information from the radio and tv, listening to what people around him are saying, picking up somebody else's newspaper or magazine and leafing through it in the office while he waits for his secretary to type a letter.

The more you know about what's affecting your audience and how they live, what's in their heads, what they long for and are fearful of, the myths they cherish, the fads and fashions they fall in and out of love with, the better off you'll be as an adperson and the fresher and brighter your ads will be.

It doesn't matter much what your major is in college if you want to become a copywriter. Major agencies don't care. They judge you primarily by the portfolio you present when you ask for a job. My advice would be to major in the subject that interests you most. In my case, it was Sociology. Many writers I know majored in Journalism, Psychology, History or English—in other words, the liberal arts. For many years, I thought my broad academic knowledge of Sociology and Psychology put me ahead of other writers who hadn't studied those subjects in college. But I soon realized that most of what I had picked up intellectually at school, other less "well-educated" writers and art directors had learned intuitively on the job.

Should You Be Reading This Book?

I was discharged from the U.S. Navy where I had served as a gunnery officer aboard the heavy cruiser U.S.S. Los Angeles, in 1960. I spent the next five years living with my parents in New Jersey and writing novels which I couldn't get published. Then I decided to try to get a copywriting job. I searched the library for books about copywriting but those I found weren't very helpful. I tried writing some ads on my own, but without guidance and direction, I got nowhere. At my wit's end, I called a former fraternity brother from Duke, a cub writer at BBDO in New York named Steve Feldman, whose father was a top creative man at Young & Rubicam. Steve asked me to dinner at his father's Westport summer home.

Steve and I spoke at length about ads and advertising. He showed me the speculative ads he'd written in order to land his job at BBDO. I thanked him profusely, but privately I wasn't sure we were getting anywhere.

On his way up to bed, Steve's father, Charlie, poked his head into the study where we were working. He looked at my samples, spread around the floor. "Why don't you put them in one of those sample books, the ones with the clear plastic pages, so it's easier to go through them?" he suggested, and continued up the stairs.

That was the extent of his help, but it came at the right time and was very important to me, because it helped give me a start. Presenting your work properly in an interview shows that at least you know *something* about looking for an ad job; shoving a bunch of loose pages at an interviewer makes you look like an amateur.

After I'd been writing copy for about a year, I wrangled an appointment with Bert Neufeld, a well-known art director turned writer who was a group head at Y&R at that time and who eventually became creative director of Wells, Rich, Greene. He looked carefully at all my work then turned back to the first page. "Garbage!" he cried. "Junk! . . . Naaa! Nobody's interested in *that,*" he added, pointing to my second headline. He went through my portfolio like a buzz saw. What he was telling me was that I had to start over. It may sound odd, but his advice, or better put, his reactions, were extremely helpful.

I once read that the average age of beginners in advertising was 27. I can't vouch for that figure, but it seems about right to me. If it is right, it means most adpeople spend five years after college or nine years after high school doing something other than advertising. A friend bummed around California after graduating from Cornell, sold brushes door to door, held a public relations job in New York for a while, drifted to and around Europe for nine months, and finally drifted into advertising. Another good friend spent ten years working in his father's clothing business hating every minute of it. He toyed with the idea of becoming a concert pianist. His father finally sold the business, throwing my friend out of work. He went to work for a small ad agency. Today he's a vice president and creative director of a well-known New York agency.

My point is that many, if not most, creative people do something else for a living before they go into the ad business. My own feeling is that the experiences they have after leaving school and before getting into the agency business make them more effective adpeople, because it teaches them a lot about what life is like outside their own hometowns, and more importantly, helps them decide what they themselves want out of the twenty-five or thirty years they're going to spend on the job.

Of course, many writers and art directors do go directly from school to an agency because they know at an early age that advertising is the kind of work they want to do. Most art directors I know have graduated from good art colleges. I'm no more familiar with these schools than I am with those schools which offer advertising courses, but what has been true in the past was that, in general, art colleges taught students to think as artists rather than salespeople. The result was graduates often knew a lot about the technical side of advertising, but very little about how to put together an ad that would sell. Usually, junior art directors use their technical training to get jobs in agency paste-up rooms or bullpens and work their way up from there.

SUMMING UP

1. Make two piles of magazine and newspaper ads—one you love and ones you hate. Study them, looking for differences and similarities in terms of headline, copy style, layout and graphic treatment.
2. Become familiar with the Red Book.
3. Buy a copy of *The One Show* book. Study the ads carefully. Compare the ads you see there with the ads you see in newspapers and magazines every day.
4. Subscribe to *Advertising Age* and *Adweek*.
5. Begin creating ads of your own and put them in a portfolio. Don't worry if they're terrible at first; they're bound to get better as you develop your skills.
6. Contact local ad agencies and try to get a part-time or summer job in one of them.
7. Read everything you can about the advertising business.
8. Ask your family and friends why they use the products they do. Talk to them about their favorite products.
9. Make an effort to become knowledgeable about popular culture—the books, movies, magazines, tv programs and celebrities people find interesting.

How to Get Your First Copywriting Job

NOTES

CHAPTER 2

BEFORE YOU WRITE YOUR OWN ADS, STUDY OTHER PEOPLE'S

Ask the people around you what they think about the ads you've collected and the commercials you see together on tv. Try to discover which ads and commercials they like and which they hate, and try to see if you can draw some tentative conclusions about advertising from their comments.

Study the movies you see on tv and in theaters. Take note of the different ways scenes can be framed and the different perspectives from which each scene could have been shot. Ask yourself why the director opened the movie the way he did. What visual tricks did he use to increase the dramatic impact of the story? Did the dialogue sound forced? Why? Ask yourself the same questions about the tv commercials you see.

SUMMING UP

1. Ask family and friends what they think of the ads in your portfolio. Don't be defensive—try to learn from their comments.
2. Study movies and tv programs, especially the longer, more ambitious dramatic programs. Ask yourself whether there is a better way to frame each scene. Study the pacing of the movie, the tone of the writing, the way it was edited. Could it have been paced differently? Pay particular attention to the sound track and lighting in movies. Could they have been more effective, more dramatic?
3. Do the same thing with tv commercials.

Before You Write Your Own Ads, Study Other People's

NOTES

CHAPTER 3

WHAT AN AD IS SUPPOSED TO DO AND HOW IT DOES IT

Imagine you are behind the counter selling merchandise on the main floor of a very large department store. Every hour hundreds, perhaps thousands, of people pass by you on the way to some other counter or floor. Perhaps they are just browsing. Imagine that you are being paid twenty dollars a week plus commission so in order to keep from starving, you've got to do some hard selling.

For the moment let us presume the item you're trying to sell is a particular brand name men's electric shaver we shall call Brand X. At nearby counters, your competitors are hawking competitive models. On the counter in front of you are several Brand X models. In the case beneath the counter are many more, along with various shaving accessories.

Time out! Come back to reality for a moment. You are sitting at your desk with the two piles of ads you love and hate in front of you. Take a few from each pile, spread them out on the desk and examine them for a few moments.

You will notice most of the ads consist of three parts—the headline in large type, the picture (an illustration or photograph), and the copy, in small type. Some ads, like the current *Marlboro* cigarette campaign, may have only a picture and the name of the product. Some ads may have no picture at all, only copy. A few ads may lack a headline. I have never yet seen an ad that was all picture without a single word of copy or type, but you may have come across one.

16

What An Ad Is Supposed To Do and How It Does It

As you can see, ads consist of three main elements; copy, headline and picture. How do they relate to each other in order to make up an effective whole? The answer is simple, if you'll imagine you're back behind the counter in the department store again. The readers of the ads correspond to the people rushing by your counter. The headline corresponds to what you would shout out to or at these customers, for example, "Hey you people, take a look at this great Brand X electric shaver!" The illustration in the ad corresponds to the Brand X shaver on the counter in front of you. The copy in the ad corresponds to the sales pitch you'd give to those passersby who were attracted by your shout and your razor and came over for a closer inspection.

That's it. Sounds simple, doesn't it? As prospective customers pass by, you shout something about your product at them. At the same time, you hold the razor in your right hand and point to it with your left in order to attract their attention to it. When they approach your counter you spend a minute or two explaining what the razor will do for them. What you shout at them is a print ad's headline; the product you show is the print ad's picture and the sales pitch you give is the ad's copy.

Obviously, the heart of the matter is the headline and picture and the way they fit together. What you say and show must attract, inform, beguile, amuse or entice your audience enough to persuade them to give you their attention. Ideally, your headline and your picture will help each other synergistically; that is, the two together will work more than twice as well as each would separately.

Remember, all around you other salespeople selling more or less comparable electric shavers will be trying to do exactly the same thing to exactly the same people. And some of them will have louder voices, bigger hands to hold their shavers, more attractive counter displays, better locations, more handsome faces, more stylish clothes, and so on.

What's more, I'm going to make your job even more difficult; in the back of the store is a sweet, innocent, old woman selling the most delicious fresh-baked rye bread for fifteen cents a loaf! She's been doing it for years and is now famous. People from all over the neighborhood flock to her counter. She's been there for a generation and many of the store's regular customers wouldn't consider it a passable week without at least one visit to her. So they are not only passing by you, they are hurrying by you and your fellow electric shaver salespeople to get to the bread woman before she runs out of rye.

In other words, your prospective customers don't give a damn about you *or* your electric razor. They couldn't care less that you only make twenty bucks a week—you, after all, are young and good-looking and have the rest of your life ahead of you, while this old woman in the back of the store has to sell all the bread she can get in order to stay out of the poorhouse. Her product is familiar and dependable and costs a couple of pennies while yours runs well over forty dollars. And her product is consumed and must be bought again, bringing her more profit, while yours will last a long time.

Let me tell you something more about your prospective customers. If yours is a more or less average department store and they are more or less average Americans, they spend their days trying to feed a family of four on something like $22,000 a year.[1] They are still paying off the loan on their old car, and when it starts to fall apart they'll begin paying off a new one. Either out of boredom, frustration or a desire to forget about their monetary problems, some member of their family sits in front of the tv set more than seven hours a day. They're worried about their health because they've been told they don't get enough exercise, eat too many fatty foods and are overweight.

The newspapers keep telling them everything they like to do is no good for them. The air is bad, the roads are bad, the chemicals in their food are dangerous. They're wondering whether some nut is going to drop a nuclear bomb on their city, or some other nut will poison the water supply, that is, if the chemical runoff from the local irrigation ditches hasn't already poisoned it.

And these poor devils are supposed to buy an electric razor from you! They already have two old electric razors somewhere in the back of a closet. Some of the men think it's virile to shave with soap and a blade and only fuzzy-cheeked college kids use electric razors. Some just don't like your face, clothes, voice or manner and wouldn't buy candles from you in a blackout. They won't tell you that, of course. They'll just give you that hostile, anonymous urban stare and hurry on—so you won't even know how to correct what you've been doing wrong.

That's pretty much what you're up against when you try to create an effective ad or commercial. If you try a rational sales approach, you must bear in mind that nearly three-quarters of your prospective customers won't even use the auto seatbelts the government has insisted be made available to them, even though car crashes kill over a thousand customers a week. If you try to entice them with a lot of artsy-craftsy talk and dextrous finger work, they may think you're weird and avoid you.

If you dress extra fancy, they're liable to think you're a sharpy and

---

[1] Latest available government figures indicate $20–$24,000 is the median income for the 78 million U.S. family units.

untrustworthy. If you don't, they'll think you're a hippy and undependable.

In any event: There are four characteristics a good headline, or headline/picture combination, should have; it should be (1) meaningful, (2) believable, (3) relevant and (4) provocative.

Since people in department stores or readers of magazines or watchers of tv programs don't have much time to spare, they won't pay much attention to a headline they don't understand immediately, or almost immediately. So your headline must be *meaningful*. You should always remember that people buy magazines for editorial, not advertising matter, and they don't turn on the tv for commercials.

If your headline isn't *believable*, even though it may attract attention, your sales pitch will be disappointing because it will not fulfill the promise made by the headline. Your readers will be offended and probably won't even wait to hear you out.

Your headline must be *relevant* in terms of the benefit the product offers the consumer. In other words, one way or another, your headline should talk about shaving—how well, or how fast or how comfortably the razor cuts hair. The shape, color, style, weight and heft of the razor are important, but they are not *the* most important aspect of your product. *How well it cuts* is what readers want to know, and that, in one form or another, is what your headline should tell them, or what it should allude to.

Provocative is a hard word to define and perhaps an impossible word to define precisely. In this context it means; interesting, exciting, humorous, fresh, imaginative, sexy, informative, unusual, compelling, bizarre, astounding, surprising, unexpected. In other words, "provocative" means anything that will gain the reader's attention in a believable, meaningful, relevant way.

As far as your Brand X shaver is concerned, you might shave a peach to show the razor shaves close without irritation, or shave a piece of carpet to show how sharp and tough its blades are. Or you might shave yourself, or a model who has just shaved a few minutes before with a blade, to show that the shaver you are selling shaves even closer than a blade. Or you might even offer to shave customers. In fact, you might even run to the back of the store and try to shave the bread woman—her large following would provide you with an instant audience.

SUMMING UP

1. Imagine you are in a large department store, on the first floor. You are trying to sell a product to customers who pass by in the aisles. What you call out to them corresponds to the headline in your ad. The picture of the product you hold up for them to see, or the product itself, corresponds to the ad's visual. What you say to them after they've come to your counter corresponds to the company.

2. What makes ads effective is the way the three elements, copy, headline and visual, relate to each other.

3. The heart of the ad is the headline/visual combination. This combination should *dramatize the benefit* the product offers the consumer. Put another way, this combination should tell a story, or begin to tell a story that dramatizes the benefit the product offers—or dramatizes the ills which may befall the consumer if he or she doesn't purchase the product.

4. A good headline/visual combination must be meaningful, believable, relevant and provocative.

NOTES

CHAPTER 4

AUDIENCES LOVE BENEFITS

The heart of any commercial or print ad is *the benefit it promises the reader or viewer.*

The reader or viewer approaches your ad, as he approaches almost everything else in life, with one question and one question only in mind: *what's in it for me?* Your ad must tell him, and quickly. It can tell him cleverly, imaginatively, emotionally, artistically or editorially, but *it must tell him—quickly.*

If you bought this book, or somebody bought it for you, it wasn't to hand over their hard won cash in order to enlarge my bank account. You bought my book because you thought it would benefit you. And that's basically why you read ads or watch commercials.

Everything in an advertisement is secondary to the benefit the advertiser promises his product will deliver if the reader does what the ad tells him to do.

A good many agencies insist that the benefit as well as the client's name be spelled out in the headline of practically every ad. Ads like that tend to be clear and to the point, but dull. These agencies argue that, since more people read headlines than copy, they might as well get the benefit up there big where everybody can and will see it before they turn the page.

Other agencies feel dull ads don't get read, and even when they do, they're not remembered and so, don't have much impact. Certainly, they feel, it is better to catch and hold the reader's attention for a longer period of time by getting him or her to read the entire ad. That way, the reader is theirs alone for as long as several minutes.

Most of the ads which have won recognition at award shows during the past fifteen years have featured neither the product benefit nor the client's name in the headline.

The headline in these ads are called "blind headlines" because the benefit is hinted at rather than spelled out; the reader must read the copy to find out what the advertiser has to offer in concrete terms. Because these ads tend to be more interesting, the theory goes, they will be more memorable—each ad in the series will stick in people's minds and in the final analysis, the ads will prove more effective.

These are the sort of ads I myself almost always try to write, the kind people find most interesting, and the kind that will get you a job in the best agencies.

I should add at this point that there are occasions when a simple, direct headline will do quite nicely. If you're trying to sell a parrot in the classified section of your local newspaper, for example, "Parrot for Sale" may be the best headline. And if your product is indeed unique and revolutionary, you may do just as well to announce that fact in the headline and let it go at that. An excellent headline for an ad announcing a cure for cancer would be, "Announcing a Cure for Cancer."

SUMMING UP

1. Every ad should offer the viewer or reader a benefit.

NOTES

CHAPTER 5

WHAT YOU NEED BESIDES ABILITY TO MAKE ADS

Now that you know what an ad is made of, you can make yourself some. Perhaps you might like to try an ad campaign. A campaign is simply three, four or five ads in a series with a common theme.

Get yourself a fiber tip pen or any other kind of writing instrument that can make a sturdy black line, an 11 × 14 (or larger) drawing pad, and a portable typewriter. Draw your own layouts, letter in your own headlines, and draw bunches of parallel lines to indicate the space to be occuppied by copy. Type out your copy on a separate sheet of paper. If you create a campaign, you need only write the copy for the first one or two ads.

If you can draw, draw your own pictures; if you can't, find somebody who can. If you can't draw, and you can't find somebody who can, *don't worry*. Draw stick figures. How good your drawings are is not important. Every agency of any size has sketch people who can draw well. Many excellent art directors are very poor renderers. Your *ideas, the way your think, the way you choose to dramatize what you want to get across,* is what is important to creative directors. There is no "rule" for layouts, just as there are no rules for anything in advertising. However, there are certain guidelines you should learn to follow. The headline can be at the bottom or the top of the ad, or it can be on the upper right hand side of the ad with the picture on the left, running down the left hand side. It can be in large or small type, short or long. It can be in caps and lower case, or all caps. It can have a period at the end or not. You can learn a lot by studying the ads you see in magazines. There are perhaps a dozen standard layouts. At another point in this book, there's a "standard" layout I suggest you use until you get the hang of making layouts.

Whatever you do, make your layout simple. And make sure your headlines have a terse quality. Don't start a headline at the top of the page, put three dots at the end of the words, and continue the rest of the headline down at the bottom. Don't write headlines on the slant—they're hard to read. Try to write simple, declarative sentences for headlines. If your headline asks a question, make that simple, too.

Most of the magazine ads you come across that seem tasteful to you will probably have very simple layouts.

TV commercials are done in a slightly different way. Usually, commercials are presented to clients in storyboard form. A storyboard is a kind of running cartoon, with from one to a dozen or more small, square pictures which simulate a tv screen, and the words that go with each picture typed below that picture. You can make up your own "storyboards" simply by drawing a parallel series of squares approximately two and a half inches wide and two inches high on a piece of typewriting paper. You might have six squares drawn on each piece of paper— use as many pieces of paper as you need for each commercial. Under each square, type or print the appropriate copy to explain that square. Write "video" immediately under the square, and verbally describe the picture. Immediately under the description, write "audio", and print what the characters in that particular picture are saying. If an unseen announcer is talking, write "VOA". That means "voice over announcer". "Voice over" means that only the person's voice is heard, and the person is not seen on the screen. On camera announcers are abbreviated "OCA" or simply "Anncr:". If you cannot draw, use stick figures to explain the visual action in each square.

If you insist on having commercials in your portfolio, but are uncomfortable with all the drawing and measuring necessary in using squares, you can simply type out a description of your commercial.

Use plain bond paper. On the upper left, single space, type the name of the product, the length of the commercial, and the fact that it's a tv spot. Write "video" on the left side of the paper and "audio" on the right. Under "video", running down the left hand side of the page, explain as simply as possible, single space, what the viewer would be seeing in each scene. Parallel to each "video" section, under "audio", on the right, double space, type out what the viewer would hear in that particular frame, and who says it ("Mom," "Pop," "Sis," etc.) Usually, a thirty-second commercial contains about 68 words. If one announcer says everything and there is no dialogue you can use more words. If several characters converse, try to keep your dialogue within the 68 or 70 word limit. These two parallel columns of type will explain quite accurately what the commercial is about.

If you can draw fairly well, and your commercial involves just one scene, you can simplify things. Just draw one large frame, perhaps four by four and a half inches, at the top of the page. Draw in your main scene. Under the picture, write "audio" and type in the audio portion.

If it's still hard for you to visualize what a tv storyboard or script looks like, check your local library. There ought to be some advertising textbooks that will give you examples of a typical script or storyboard. If your college has an advertising department, check with them. I'm sure they'll be able to supply you with an example.

Because of high time costs, most commercials today are written in 30 second rather than 60 second lengths. You will have to time your commercial to make sure the audio portion will fit into the allotted time period. Thirty-second commercials usually contain no more than 25 seconds of copy.

The "concept" of a print ad (the idea behind the execution of the sales message, or, thought of in another way, the unique combination of headline and layout) applies to tv commercials as well, but in a slightly different way. More on this later.

Unlike a print ad, a commercial is linear and the audience has no control over its presentation. In other words, a reader can linger over a print ad, repeating various parts to himself and studying the picture or pictures until he gets the message. When he watches a tv commercial, what happens in the last few seconds, and whether it makes any sense to him, depends completely upon what happened in the first seconds; each scene builds on itself and on the scene before, to tell a kind of mini-story. If the viewer doesn't perceive steps A,B,C, and D, he or she certainly isn't going to make heads or tails of steps E,F,G, and H; he or she can't reread the copy, and he or she can't review the picture.

So a commercial must be even more concise and tightly constructed than a print ad. Naturally, the concept or idea of the commercial is not quite the same as the headline/picture combination in a print ad. For the time being, you can think of the concept of a commercial as the little story or executional gimmick the authors have used to get the sales message across.

A zipper commercial once featured a fictional "great escape artist" who had just escaped from beneath a river though bound by what looked like a ton of chains. But while he was being interviewed, he couldn't quite make it out of his wetsuit, presumably because it wasn't equipped with the client's zipper. The humorous vignette was used to get the point across in a lighthearted way that the client's zippers are superior to, or at least more dependable than ordinary zippers.

To show how much faith women have in a certain brand of detergent, an agency concocted a series of commercials which showed a man offering women who had already bought the sponsor's product two boxes of a competitive detergent for one box of their favorite. The women who refused the two for one offer were used in commercials.

Another campaign was based upon interviewing housewives who had *not* used the sponsor's product once in the past and had had a disastrous experience as a result.

Using a personality or celebrity in a campaign can be an excellent idea, if those celebrities are used imaginatively and their appearance is given some sort of fresh, unexpected twist.

A classic Volkswagen commercial showed a Volkswagen being driven out of a garage on a snowy night and off into the distance. Near the end of the commercial, the off-screen announcer said, "Have you ever wondered how the man who *drives* a snowplow drives *to* the snowplow? This one drives a Volkswagen, so you can stop wondering." The idea was that the Volkswagen's rear wheel drive provides superior traction in snow because most of the car's weight is on the driving wheels.

Many commercials consist of a male or female announcer extolling the virtues of the product in front of the camera. These spots tend to be dull. Still more involve the use of a side-by-side demonstration showing the superiority of the sponsor's product when tested against a competitive brand.

It's sometimes difficult to know exactly what the art director and writer contributed to a given commercial, especially those for food products, because so much of the impact of the final piece of film depends upon so-called "production values"—that is, fancy artistic touches provided by the production company, the director and the actors. A good director working with responsive actors can sometimes make a run-of-the-mill commercial come alive. For example, when you think about it, there aren't many facts a writer can pack into a food commercial. Food is food; either it tastes good or it doesn't; it's convenient to prepare or it isn't; it's nutritious or it isn't. It's impossible to prove that one food tastes better than another, since taste is subjective. That's why food commercials are often among the most artfully produced commercials you'll see on tv. Children are often used very effectively in food commercials.

I'll have more to say about commercials in another chapter. Many factors over which the authors have little or no control affect tv commercials, including the amount of money the client is willing to spend to produce them. A clever tv idea in your portfolio is a clever tv idea, but there's no way for a prospective employer to know how it will turn out without getting a lot of other people involved. So while it's not a bad idea to have some tv ideas, campaigns and storyboards in your portfolio, beginners tend to be judged more by their print than their tv. For one thing, you can present a print ad almost exactly as you want it to appear, which you can't do for tv without film. For another, few beginners even in the largest agencies get to work on tv commercials right away. Since they're usually assigned to write trade ads, a future boss wants to see what kind of print ads a beginner can do.

Of course, some writers or art directors are primarily tv-oriented by nature. If this is the case with you, by all means take advantage of your inclination and put lots of tv into your portfolio. But I would suggest you get the hang of creating good print ads first.

SUMMING UP

1. An ad *campaign* is simply three to five ads in a series with a common theme. Usually, the layouts are quite similar.
2. Try to make your layouts simple.
3. If you don't draw well, don't worry. Use stick figures.
4. If you want to have tv storyboards in your portfolio, and can't draw, and don't like stick figures, type out a description of the commercial. Keep it short and to the point.

NOTES

CHAPTER 6

THE CONCEPT: WHAT AD MAKING IS ALL ABOUT

I have referred to the concept of an ad as the entity, composed of the headline and picture combination, that makes each ad unique. That's true, but it's not quite the whole truth. The best way to define what I mean by "concept" as it relates to ad making is by example.

Let's say you come up with the theme line for a campaign for *People* magazine that says, "If you don't like the people you're with, try ours." You use that as a tag line at the bottom of each ad. As illustrations, you show photographs of people escaping from unpleasant social situations by reading *People* magazine; i.e., a man sitting in a subway car surrounded by tough-looking characters; an attractive young woman at a cocktail party or museum surrounded by a bunch of gossiping old biddies; a scrawny convict squeezed into the corner of his small prison cell by a burly cellmate, and so on.

The concept is that you can mentally escape from unpleasant situations by losing yourself in this interesting magazine, or put another way, that this magazine is so compelling that it would hold your interest even in a situation that made you nervous or fearful. Or, put a third way, "escape from people with *People*."

Let us say you are trying to persuade readers to bring their families to New York City for vacation. The concept for your campaign might be, "See the world without ever leaving the country." The idea would be that New York City is such a cosmopolitan place that you can see a bit of many other countries here without having to pay the high price of an overseas flight.

Since tv is primarily a visual medium, the concept behind a successful commercial is often strongly visual. A commercial produced some years ago for *American Tourister* luggage showed a suitcase being tossed around violently by a gorilla inside a cage. The copy went something like: Dear clumsy bellboys, brutal cab drivers. Careless doormen. Ruthless porters. Have we got a suitcase for you. *American Tourister.*

Let's go through the steps the writer and art director went through creating this superb commercial. The benefit was the ruggedness of the luggage. The question was, how could that ruggedness be demonstrated in a dramatic, memorable way? The answer was to show the suitcase surviving a bout with a 500-pound gorilla. But there's a lot more to it than that. In order for this concept to work perfectly, the visual had to be supported with exactly the right amount of the right kind of copy.

Overly dramatic, corny copy ("Ladies . . . and gentlemen! . . . In this corner . . . a five hundred pound gorilla! . . . In the corner with him, an *American Tourister* suitcase!") would detract from the visual. Flat, semi-documentary copy (". . . we put this rugged *American Tourister* suitcase in a gorilla's cage. Watch what happened to it. Nothing . . .") would work better. But it wouldn't really help the commercial come alive. The actual copy, written in the form of a letter, is terse and not overly wordy, so it doesn't compete for attention with the visual. At the same time, it brings a new dimension to the commercial because the casual, almost laconic tone of the copy provides ironic counterpoint to the visual.

It's easy to understand the definition of a concept in terms of vacation resorts, magazines, luggage or small appliances. But there are products that offer the consumer a more subtle benefit, which is much harder to define, demonstrate or differentiate from the benefits offered by competitors. Perfume, men's cologne, the taste of Coke, 7-UP or Pepsi, or the services of a bank or an airline fall into this category.

Are you familiar with the Marlboro cigarette campaign? Each ad consists of a magnificent photograph of a cowboy, usually in action on a horse. There is a no copy, except for the product name in large type.

What is the concept? Well, although there are some distinct differences between cigarette brands, most brands apparently taste pretty much the same. So, what sells cigarettes in the images created for them by ad agencies. People like to smoke a cigarette whose "personality" fits their own, or what they'd like to think is their own.

The Marlboro ads create a virile personality for the cigarette. They imply that strong, individualistic, aggressive, hard working, down to earth men (or women, for that matter) prefer Marlboro. No copy is necessary; the pictures say it all. This concept sounds pretty dull until you see it executed. As a matter of fact, in this case, the concept and the execution are really one and the same thing, since the execution, not the concept, is what is truly unique and original.

This is often true with parity products like beer, whiskey, cigarettes and soft drinks or the services of a bank or an airline.

United Airlines' theme line is "Fly the friendly skies of United." Their splendidly produced tv commercials show friendly employees and customers flying United.

In United's case, the concept of their campaign is inherent in the production values displayed in the commercials. Basically, all they do is try to leave you with a nice, positive feeling about United. They attempt to create a personality for, or personalize United. They don't high pressure you and they don't editorialize. They're almost pure emotion. Are they successful? Yes, indeed. If a jingle seems like a trivial reason to pick one airline over another, remember that many buying decisions, even those involving high priced items like cars, houses and clothes, involve equally emotional or at least non-rational motivation. Besides, people don't really pick an airline because they like its song; the song is merely a way to keep the airline's name in people's minds, so that, when they have to fly, they're likely to call that airline.

Sometimes concepts that appear to lack concrete substance are actually loaded with symbolic significance. BMW's tag line, "The Ultimate Driving Machine" is a good example. There's a "macho" quality to this particular choice of words that's hard for most men to resist. The words imply that BMW automobiles are more than mere *cars*—they're "driving machines," built for highly sophisticated drivers . . . virile, knowledgeable, *serious* drivers interested in high performance and high quality.

Sometimes, especially on tv, the concept, as such, is so thin, it's almost invisible. Many subtle factors are involved in communication through film. The way a set is dressed, the product lit, the inflection in the announcer's voice, the melody or lyrics of a song, the personality of the celebrity on camera—all these things can be classified as part of the concept. Even the graphic treatment of the logo (the identifying mark or symbol the client uses to mark his product or company) can be part of the concept.

In other words, a concept can consist of almost anything—a performance, a statement, a picture, a way of filming, a snippet of sound or talk, a dramatic or humorous bit of stage business, a disguised sexual reference. But basically *a concept is an advertising idea which allows a product benefit, which is either inherent or imparted, to be dramatized for the consumer in a unique, compelling, provocative way.*

The concept can take concrete or symbolic form in a campaign theme line, in a headline/picture combination, mainly in the graphics or "look" of an ad or campaign, mainly in what the headline or copy says, in the feeling-tone communicated by two people who talk to each other on camera or to the audience, or in the way a celebrity is presented.

Most campaign concepts are more or less arrived at intuitively by an art director/writer team. These people don't necessarily sit at their desks making lists of psychological motivations and plotting ways to make use of them. They simply let their minds wander. The question they try to answer is basically a simple one: exactly who are we talking to and how can we gain their attention? Very often, they come up with something more or less by accident, or so it seems. Actually, they are making use of their unconscious minds—the impulses, desires, hopes and fears they share with their audience.

I hope what I've written up to this point attempting to illustrate and clarify what I mean by "concept" is clear. No doubt for many readers it will be, and they might as well skip to the end of this chapter. But I know from my teaching experience at The School of Visual Arts that many people will still be confused.

So let me try another example.

Suppose you're advertising a new brand of frozen fishsticks. The strategy is to convince consumers that, unlike most brands, these fishsticks really do taste like freshly caught fish. "Fresh caught taste" is an abstraction. In order to get people to respond emotionally to abstractions, you have to give them concrete forms. In other words, you have to dramatize your point of view or message—just as writers, artists and sculptors have done for centuries.

In this case, you have to come up with some sort of executional device (concept) that demonstrates fresh taste, or fresher taste than the competition. There are many ways of doing it. You could show your fishsticks alongside a freshly caught fish. You could simply show a fresh fish with a provocative headline. You could educate the consumer about how fish are caught, how they're processed and why yours are better. You could interview the president of the fish company and write an ad about him. Maybe his family has been in the fish business for a hundred years. Maybe they have a fetish about freshness. Maybe they spend millions of dollars on refrigerated trucks to keep their fish fresh on the way to the cannery. (It doesn't matter, incidentally, if his competitors do the same things he does; if he advertises and they don't, consumers will believe he does beneficial things to his products and they don't). In your ads, you could show a still life of a rod and reel, the ocean, a fishing boat, a delivery truck, or a fisherman. You could write an all copy ad with a headline like "At last—fishsticks for people who've sworn off fishsticks." A restaurant near my office has a sign painted on the wall that reads, "The fish you eat today, slept last night in Chesapeake Bay".

There's no end of word/picture combinations you can dream up to get the point across that your fishsticks are truly fresher-tasting. It may take some digging on your part. When I was putting my first portfolio together, I spent hours pouring over books and magazines in the public library. As I've said elsewhere, the more you know about your product and how it's made, the more grist you have for your creative mill.

Now then. Let's assume you have a very good idea of what an advertising concept is, creatively speaking. Let us say you have a perfect understanding of just how important concepts are to copywriters and art directors. I shall now contradict myself, and no doubt utterly confuse many of my most attentive readers, by pointing out that you can sometimes create quite effective advertising without much of a concept.

Mixtures of moving visual images and songs can profoundly touch people's emotions in ways an audience cannot explain. It's an inherent power unique to film. To an extent, the stage shares that power. Many shows which aren't about much of anything are rightfully called "great theater."

Gone With the Wind and *The Wizard of Oz* are classics for reasons that have little to do with what they have to say to mankind. *Casablanca* is wonderful to watch for all sorts of reasons that have more to do with the dialogue, the actors, the direction and the pacing of the movie than with the message or point of view of the screenwriter.

Sometimes, certain sequences in films are very powerful simply because they touch deep wellsprings of emotion. Gene Kelly's "Singing in the Rain" sequence from the movie of the same name, is one. Another is the opening sequence of the movie, *Patton*. George C. Scott, as

37

the iconoclastic, charismatic, controversial general, strides back and forth giving a speech to his troops. He is festooned with ribbons and medals and he wears his famous pearl-handled Colt 45 revolver. Behind him is an immense American flag. The highlight of his speech occurs when he tells the troops, ". . . I want you to remember, no bastard ever won a war by dying for his country . . . he won it by making the *other poor dumb bastard* die for his country . . ." When Scott leaves the screen, he leaves the audience breathless. Most of them are not sure whether they're supposed to love, hate or fear the man. They're not sure what the filmmakers mean to make of Patton. But they are convinced he's a fascinating man, and they want to know more about him.

The current Wheaties campaign, "What the Big Boys Eat", is a perfect example of the "execution is concept" phenomenon. What the commercials say, in effect, is that Wheaties are what active people enjoy eating. But the delightful, joyous *way* it is said leaves the audience with good feelings about the product and the healthful effects of eating it. There's also an implication that "big boys"—professional athletes and particularly strong, healthy people interested in good health and fine bodies and so forth—eat Wheaties. When the commercials end, you feel good about Wheaties without quite knowing why.

In my experience, this sort of executional brilliance cannot be taught, at least not to beginners. And even if beginners understood it they could not demonstrate it in their portfolios, since they don't have either the experience or the facilities to create beautifully finished commercials. So as a practical matter, there's not much point in dwelling on tv spots like these, since they're beyond the scope of this book.

On the other hand, no book attempting to teach people about advertising creativity would be complete without at least mentioning this "other kind" of creativity, this "other kind of good advertising." It is creativity that has little or nothing to do with logic or concepts, necessarily, but which comes from the gut and depends for its powerful effects on brilliant music, skillful choreography and splendid filmmaking.

SUMMING UP

1. The *concept* is the executional gimmick, idea, premise or device you have thought of to dramatize the benefit your product offers.
2. An effective concept does not necessarily have to have a great deal of concrete substance. It can have considerable *symbolic* significance, but may still appear, on the surface, to be rather trivial, even silly. Some concepts are brash and bold, others are more tasteful and restrained. Neither kind is better; the best concept is the one most appropriate for the product.

NOTES

CHAPTER 7

HOW TO GO ABOUT THINKING UP GOOD ADS

Dreaming up good ads involves two processes—one public, one private.

As previously discussed, the success of the public process depends upon keeping yourself tuned into the activities and events around you— radio and tv programs, the conversations of friends, newspaper columns and so forth.

The private process involves the ability to develop your own unique creative potential. There has never been another person in the world exactly like you, and there never will be again. When you create an ad, you must use your individual attributes to create a fresh, original piece of work that will communicate to the unique individuals in your audience. There's nothing mysterious about this process; it goes on all the time with comedians, teachers, scriptwriters and politicians. The comedian makes up a joke based upon a common bond of shared experiences, and a new twist to an old insight or a new way of looking at the same old things. His jokes won't work if his audience isn't "with him", if it doesn't understand his view of life or sympathize with the role he plays. And they won't work if the audience has heard them before—if the comedian's particular view of life, as it's communicated in his material, isn't fresh.

There is no single best way to write ads. Everybody has his or her own style. But there are some suggestions most beginners find helpful.

First, as I've mentioned before, learn all you can about the product you're writing about. Read ads about it, if you can find some. Ask people who have used it what they think of it. Go to the library and do some research. If it's a perfume, learn all you can about perfume in general. If you're going to write about auto tires, read what *Consumer Reports* tests say about tires.

When you've learned all you can, isolate yourself in a quiet room. In as few words as possible, write down exactly what you want to say about the product. In other words, in one short, declarative sentence, tell your audience what this product does for them. Keep this statement handy as a reference as long as you're working on the product. Make yourself comfortable, close your eyes and let your mind wander. Think about those times when you or somebody you knew used the product in the past, or a product like it. What were these people like? What did they get out of using the product? Under what conditions did they use it? What happened when they did? What would have happened if they didn't? If you had asked them why they bought it, what would they have told you? If you wanted a friend to try the product, what would you tell him? What statement would you make about the product to attract his attention? If you were writing a friend a letter about the product, what would you tell him about it?

Keep a pad and pencil in your lap while you write down headlines, statements, puns, word plays, situations where the product might be used, etc. After you've done this awhile, think of a visual for your ad and write twenty or thirty headlines to go with it.

Think up another visual and write ten or fifteen more headlines. Compare the visuals and headlines. Forget about a visual and just write headlines, perhaps twenty or twenty-five. They can be statements of fact, questions, one or two word exclamations, 16 word declarations, anything. There are no rules.

Try to think up an ad without any words. What pictures come to mind involving the product or people in a situation where they might find it helpful?

Think in negative terms. Under what circumstances would a consumer never be likely to need or use this product? What negative headlines can you think of? Try saying something shocking about the product in a headline—something no newspaper or magazine would ever print.

When the fantasizing begins to become fatiguing, stop. Leave the room and do something else to occupy your mind—eat, ski, read, talk, shoot a bow and arrow, play golf, polish furniture, fly a kite. After a few minutes or hours or days of that, try thinking of visuals and writing headlines or tv commercials while you watch tv, listen to the radio or talk with friends.

By the end of the day or after several days you should have several pages covered with headlines and visual ideas. Start sketching the pictures, printing the headlines and indicating copy with bunches of parallel lines. You'll convert several pages of lines into several pages of ads. When you've finished, put them aside for a couple of days. Attend to other business. Try to forget about advertising. You mind will be working on ads whether or not you think it is. Get in the habit of carrying a paper and pencil with you and jot down ideas for new ads as they come to you.

Take a fresh look at your original ads. Chances are, many that looked good in the first place don't excite you anymore. If you're getting sick and tired of the product you're working on, begin ads for several others.

Take a walk, see a movie, play ball, do anything not overtly connected with your assignment. Don't get discouraged. Sometimes, you won't come up with anything for hours or even days. Sometimes, you'll discover you can't make yourself care about a product anymore. Forget about it and go on to something else, perhaps to some product or service that interests you very much. Or try forcing yourself into the opposite routine; pick a product you couldn't possibly use yourself, one you haven't the slightest interest in, and do ads about it. If you're a man, write about lingerie or perfume, and if you're a woman, write about after-shave lotion or men's underwear.

At first, it will take a lot of willpower to learn to work the way I've suggested. After a while, you may feel a little silly doing so much soul searching about such unimportant subjects as mouthwash, sunburn remedies, denture adhesives and floor cleaners. But it will seem more natural after you've done it for a while. What I'm suggesting you do, after all, is simply what experienced ad makers do in a much more casual and unself-conscious way.

An exercise many students find helpful is to search through newspapers for interesting photos, tear them out, and try to write headlines for them. You can tear out any sort of picture and try to make it work in an ad for any sort of product. It's not a good way for a professional to create an ad—I find that starting with a specific picture in mind usually hampers me—but it's an excellent idea for beginners because it forces writers to think visually and art directors to think verbally. And there's no end to superb pictures in the magazines around your home. By the way, old magazines like *Life* and *Look* are excellent for this purpose.

Another helpful activity is to study the captions in newspapers and headlines at the top of editorial and feature stories. The titles of each months' articles are always published on the *Reader's Digest's* front cover. Many of those titles make excellent headlines. They have to, since they act as advertisements for the magazine when travelers browsing in train stations or at airport newstands pick it off the rack. In fact, placing the table of contents on the front cover is an excellent way to encourage people to pick up the magazine in the first place.

The most important advice I can give you when you actually sit down to create ads and commercials is, *for God's sake don't be too rational.* That's what free association is all about—write down whatever comes to mind. The wackier your thoughts, the better. When you create an ad, you're trying to plumb the depths of your own unconscious. Your unconscious is what *you* are all about—the heart, the core, the wellspring of your creative power. Don't sell your unconscious short by being too rational or self-critical in your approach.

This is especially true when it comes to those products I mentioned in the previous chapter, (whose distinctive consumer benefits are hard to define precisely,) such as beer, cigarettes, airlines and soft drinks. There is no logical, purely rational way to convince consumers that Coke tastes better than Pepsi or Marlboro is a better tasting cigarette than Camels. What these advertisers are looking for is an *idea;* a visual gimmick, a cute phrase, a visual device, a jingle, a vignette, a bit of business, a certain look, a catchy phrase—something that will stick in the minds of viewers and readers and remind them of the brand when they're about to buy a product in that category.

I repeat, when you're writing ads, let yourself think weird, crazy, far out thoughts. They're often the basis of good ads. More important, they're part of an unfettered frame of mind, an open door to your own imaginative powers, that will prevent you from thinking in stale, stereotyped ways.

Have you ever been thrilled by an operatic aria, a painting, a descriptive passage in a novel or poem, or an actor's performance? Surely you have been moved to tears on occasion by a book or movie. Instead of moving people to tears, advertising attempts to move them to buy or believe. It seeks to touch their emotions and by doing so, makes them think buying will somehow make their lives better. Ads that get beneath people's skin are good ads. They may appear trivial, frivolous or simple-minded to an objective observer, but your job as a product's advocate is to keep people in your audience from becoming *objective* observers. You want to make them *committed* observers. That means you have to become committed yourself, at least temporarily.

Sometimes the best way to do this is to hit them over the head with a simple, dramatic statement or picture. At other times you must charm them, entice them with images and symbols that have only an oblique connection with your product, and perhaps no overt connection with it. It's tough, because you have only a few seconds to catch and hold their attention. But you're in a lot better position than the man behind the counter in the department store. You have the finest artists, photographers, engravers, actors, directors, set designers and producers to help you—or at least you will have when you get a copywriting job.

SUMMING UP

1. There is no one best way to write good ads. Each writer or art director has his own "best" way.
2. Generally speaking, the best way to start is by learning all you can about the product.
3. One good way to work, for many copywriters, is simply to free associate—think about the product and it's uses and benefits and write down every thought for a headline and visual that comes into your head. You may not come up with anything great, but at least it's a start.
4. Don't be afraid to think in negative terms. What would happen if the consumer didn't buy the product? Sometimes a negative or unfortunate situation is easier to dramatize than a positive one. Often, it is funnier and more interesting.
5. Work for an hour at a time, or 45 minutes, then rest. Concentrate on something else to refresh your mind.
6. As an exercise, try writing your own headlines as captions to interesting photographs you cut out of the daily newspaper. You won't necessarily be creating ads, as such, but it may help put your mind in the right groove.
7. Study the headlines for articles on the front cover of *Reader's Digest*. Many of them make great headlines.
8. Try not to be too rational when you're dreaming up ads. Trust, and tap the child in yourself. Take risks. Creating highly provocative ads that are a bit obscure is not the world's worst sin. When creating advertising, the worst sin is boring people. And the next worst sin is boring yourself.

NOTES

CHAPTER 8

MISTAKES TO AVOID

The worst mistake nearly all beginners (and many professionals) make is to take criticism personally. Always remember, you are you, your work is your work. Personal involvement is characteristic of all creative work, and it's impossible for many artists to separate themselves from their work. But ad makers are not artists; they are craftsmen paid to exercise their skill on behalf of an agency's clients. Criticism of your ads is not necessarily criticism of your ability or your worth as a person. Ads are killed, but ad makers live on, up to a point. As a beginner you must be prepared to accept criticism gracefully, not personally. That's usually not too hard if you happen to agree with your critic; it's when you don't, when you think he's talking through his hat, that you have to be especially diplomatic. Your impulse will be to *tell him* that he doesn't know what he's talking about. Don't. Just don't ask his opinion a second time.

Another common mistake is to write a headline that tells the reader something he already knows. In a very basic sense, ads are news, and good ads are news, or contain news of interest to the reader. If your ad doesn't contain some news value, *some unexpected, surprising quality,* it's going to be dull. To avoid that, you have to word your headline so as to imply the reader has something new to learn by reading your ad— whether or not he really has.

48

Mistakes To Avoid

Some products are newsy by their very nature—books, magazines, newspapers, tv programs. But some, like banks and the services they provide, brokerage houses, many kinds of food and certain famous products that have been around for generations, are hard to talk about in an interesting way. It's up to the copywriter and art director to *make* these products interesting to read about. There is no excuse for a dull ad, especially in a beginner's portfolio.

When you are putting your portfolio together, it is better to err on the side of freshness and wit than dullness. If you present some ads that are clever but slightly off-target or unrealistic in a marketing sense, that's not too bad. But it *is* bad to fill your portfolio with a lot of ordinary, safe, sound ads that are right on target but dull. Creative directors have plenty of old hands around who can turn out all the dull ads they want as fast as they're wanted. What they want from a beginner is something fresh, hip, flippant, exciting, unordinary. Headlines can be long or short, they can be questions or declarative statements, mini-editorials or quick shouts, they can tell a joke or be serious, can instruct or edify, but above all, the headline and the picture that accompanies it, the concept you have decided upon, must intrigue the reader into reading your copy.

In trying to make their ads provocative, many beginners wind up with headlines that are unintelligible. It's a natural mistake. The more clever you sometimes try to be, the more obtuse you become. A good headline must be intelligible immediately, or almost immediately. A headline with an element of mystery will intrigue me, but too much mystery will confuse and irritate me. As I have pointed out before, most of the best headlines are somewhat "blind". But in most cases, the first three or four lines of the copy explain them, if not completely, at least to the point where the reader gets the general idea.

The only way I know of to learn to approach the fine line between a provocative ad and an unintelligible one is to write a lot of ads. It's best if you write them under supervision, but if you can't, write them and show them to your family and friends. If they begin to question you about the meaning of your headline/picture combination instead of trying to find the answer in the copy, the chances are, your headline is confusing.

SUMMING UP

1. Learn to fight the impulse to take criticism of your ads personally. As a professional, you must separate yourself, and your own sense of worth, from your work. It isn't easy, but it's a must.
2. Ads are news—your ads should have a *newsy, unexpected, surprising* quality about them.
3. The headlines in your headline/visual combination can be long, short, serious, happy, profound, witty, instructive, edifying, whatever. There are no rules. There are no rules for the visuals, either.

NOTES

CHAPTER 9

HELPFUL HINTS

If you're enterprising, you can find all sorts of interesting subjects to advertise. Look in your local newspaper for interesting feature stories about local businesses. Two pieces I came across recently in *The Wall Street Journal* concern a new overnight sleeper service offered by Amtrak (July 2, 1985, ''Why I Slept in Penn Station for (Just) $78.50,'' by Daniel Machalaba) and a truly fascinating piece, also in the *Journal* of the same date (front page, ''A Las Vegas Casino Welcomes Customers Its Competitors Shun'' by Bill Johnson) about Binion's Horseshoe Hotel & Casino.

You may read about certain ''rules'' to follow when creating ads. My advice would be to ignore them. There are guidelines to follow, but like life itself, advertising has no ''rules'' as such. One mythical ''rule'' is that ''showing the product in use'' is usually helpful in an ad. Forget that. *Simply try to tell a story, or begin to tell a story with your headline and layout, that dramatizes or begins to dramatize, the product benefit—or the misfortune that will follow if the reader fails to use the product.*

While you're trying to dream up such a story, you may get carried away and start to write things that are not to the point. If you find that happening, stop, put your pencil down, close your eyes, and think a moment about the ad you've just written. Open your eyes, study your ad, and ask yourself if your headline/visual combination answers the question, or at least begins to answer the question, "I should buy this product or service because . . ." in, say, a dozen words. If you can't finish that sentence with that many words, change the headline/visual combination.

Once you have determined, in as few words as possible, why somebody should buy the product, perhaps it may help to write those words out and tape them on the wall near your typewriter or drawing pad. Your job is to *dramatize* the reason why somebody should buy the product. Once you understand what it is to dramatize something, you begin to understand how silly talk of "advertising rules" is.

There are millions of ways to dramatize any statement, any theme, any point of view. Dramatists each have a unique style, as novelists, poets, painters and sculptors do. You will develop a certain characteristic style of expressing yourself as you learn to write headlines and copy.

You may be told that billboards—large outdoor billboards—usually should contain no more than seven words. That's true, generally. But I know that the moment I write that, some budding genius somewhere will come up with an award-winning billboard with seventy-five words.

You may hear the phrase, "Eighty-five percent of the people never read the body copy". When I was an *Advertising Age* columnist, I tried for weeks to track down the origin of that statement. I couldn't find it. I think it's one of those "truisms" that simply has no basis in fact. Think about it. Eighty-five percent of *what* people? Kids? Old people? Middle class people, rich people, poor people, readers, non-readers? And what kind of ads? People read automobile ads because Americans in general find cars interesting. They tend not to read corporate ads, because such ads don't promise an immediate and concrete benefit. Women read certain categories of ads with great interest; men read certain other kinds of ads with great interest.

Besides, if eighty-five percent of the people are not reading the copy, it's probably because the headline/visual combinations don't interest them enough. The trouble may not be lousy copy, but lousy headline/visual combinations.

It stands to reason more people will notice an ad than will read it, and more people will read the headline, which is much larger than the copy. But beyond those rather self evident generalizations, there's really nothing you can say regarding percentages of people who do or do not read copy that makes any sense. Write your copy as though you expect people to read it. If you're a good enough ad maker, many will.

Most published copy is far too long. It could be much shorter and more to the point. But there's no such thing as a "rule" that long copy or short copy is better. The copy should be as long as it has to be, no longer, like a joke. There are comedians who tell long jokes and those who tell short jokes. There's no such thing as a *best* kind of joke. A joke is, what a joke is. An ad is an ad, is an ad, is an ad. Good ads, like good visuals and good headlines, come in all shapes, tones, and sizes.

Ad writing should be fun. It should be exciting. Do not try to build a portfolio of ads for products you yourself find dull, or wouldn't want. Try to pick products for which you have some enthusiasm.

You may read copywriting manuals, or biographies of well-known ad people which tell you "nobody buys from clowns," or "humor doesn't sell." Nothing could be further from the truth. Those humorous commercials or ads that communicate in a provocative fashion, are good commercials.

You may read that headlines that ask a question are either more or less effective than other kinds. Nonsense. Good ads with headlines that ask questions are good ads. Bad ads with headlines that ask questions are bad ads. The only questions worth asking are: Is the headline/visual provocative? Will the reader want to read the rest of the ad?

Some headlines are complete sentences, with a period at the end. Some are not. Good headlines, like good ads, can come in all shapes, sizes and lengths.

I tell students that, generally speaking, they should not write ads for fashion items for use in their portfolios. Speaking broadly, fashion items are sold on their looks. Fashion advertising is a special area of advertising. People with an instinct for it tend to make up their own rules as they go along. Some of them are brilliant at it. But fashion ads generally are not very useful in the average job-hunter's portfolio. Or, put another way, they are not as useful as ads for other kinds of products.

Print ads for products like beer, soft drinks and cigarettes are also generally not as useful as ads for other products. The first two categories are usually advertised on tv, and backed by immense budgets, in the $30 million to $60 million range. Relatively little is spent in print media to advertise them. Cigarettes are much too controversial, in my opinion, and your time would be better spent creating ads for other types of products. Mind you, I'm not saying *"don't!"* If you absolutely love writing cigarette ads and campaigns, by all means do it. If you love writing beer and soft drink ads, write them. Just bear in mind that it's very hard for beginners to impress people with their ads and campaigns for those products.

Don't try to write ads when you're tired or preoccuppied. Writing ads is enormously draining and takes great concentration. Go at it when you can give it your best, and stop when you feel yourself getting tired.

SUMMING UP

1. Look through the daily newspaper for products to advertise. Sometimes they turn up in news stories.
2. There are no ''rules'' for creating good ads. You should regard anybody who presents you with a series of ''rules'' with great skepticism.
3. More than anything else, ads are stories about product benefits. Everybody loves good stories.
4. Most libraries contain bound volumes of back issues of *Consumer Reports,* the independent magazine that tests consumer products. Consumers Union does not depend on advertising for its revenue. Back issues of CU can make you an instant expert in scores of consumer product categories. Generally speaking, the more information you have, the better your ads will be. The December issue is published as a year-end paperback compilation of the previous 11 month's articles. If the magazine is not available locally, write: *Consumers Reports,* Consumers Union of U.S. Inc, 256 Washington St., Mount Vernon, NY 10553.

Helpful Hints

NOTES

CHAPTER 10

HOW TO WRITE THE COPY

Learning to write superb copy takes intensive training; writing passable copy, copy good enough to get you a job, isn't difficult if you've done a bit of formal writing on your own. As I've said before, it's not much different, basically, from writing a letter to a friend. The difference is, as an adperson, your "letter" concerns only one subject and it doesn't ramble the way most letters do.

To begin with, copy should be brief and to the point, with a definite beginning, middle and end. You should try to say what you have to say in the fewest posssible words. In that respect, ad copy is a lot like newspaper copy. But since your ads attempt to persuade rather than merely inform, ad copy must have much more impact and must involve the reader more than straight news copy does. In effect, you have to write your ad as though the news you have is of great interest to the reader, whether it really is or not. The news you're giving him or her is news of a product benefit. The trouble is, there just isn't that much that's new and interesting to most readers about most products. So your job is to make it *seem* as though there is. Ad copy, as opposed to news copy, must be as dramatic, vivid and compelling as you can make it. It must have a personality and style all its own. (I don't mean it must shout and boast like a side-show barker. The most persuasive copy often seems casual and friendly).

How To Write the Copy

The first couple of lines of your copy should have fairly direct (and nearly always immediate) reference to the headline. They should amplify or explain it, and at the same time act as a bridge to the body of the copy—the part that contains your sales message. As a general rule, it pays to get to the product's name and benefit fairly quickly. The product is what you're selling, after all, and its benefit is what your ad is about, so it doesn't pay to dawdle.

The final portion of your copy usually contains some sort of "call to action". By a call to action I don't mean something as bald as "run down to your corner drugstore now". If you're a good craftsman, the reader may not even be aware he's being subjected to anything as crass as a call to action.

These days, most copy winds up with a humorous or clever last line; often that line refers back to the headline. Writers sometimes spend hours thinking up clever last lines. I'm inclined to think it's an affectation, but that doesn't matter; much of the best copy written today ends that way, so you might as well learn to do it.

When you write copy, write as though you're speaking to only one person, not a group, and use simple, declarative statements. Use short sentences where you can, but avoid piling one paragraph on top of another so your copy doesn't sound choppy. In other words, vary the length of your sentences, as people do when they talk. If your copy sounds natural when read aloud, you're probably on the right track.

Try to avoid parenthetical phrases and dependent clauses. They tend to slow things up. Good copywriting, like most good writing, should have a smooth, easy, rhythm that sounds natural. It should not sound stiff, or formal or fancy. It shouldn't seem as though you labored over it. Of course, the way to achieve that effect is to labor over it.

A word of caution. In certain cases, the copy for a product may purposely *want* to sound somewhat aloof or formal. In certain situations that particular style may be more convincing. I'm not arguing that *all* copy should be written *only one way,* but rather that, as a beginner, your basic approach should be to write in a more casual, conversational style than the style you have probably learned to use in school.

The best and fastest way to learn to write copy is to write ads in an agency, under supervision. However, if you don't have a job as a copywriter, you have to train yourself, at least to the point where you can write copy that's good enough to get you a job. The easiest way to learn to write good copy is to study the copy in the ads which are listed as finalists in *The One Show* book. There's nothing dishonest about that; nearly all writers begin learning to write by imitating others.

If you own or can borrow a tape recorder, record the sound tracks of a dozen commercials and transcribe them. You'll notice a number of similarities. Although some thirty-second commercials contain only a few words of copy, most run to a maximum of about 68 words. Generally speaking, tv scripts follow the same guidelines as print copy. They too have a beginning, middle and end. And they tend to mention the product and its benefit early on. Since tv is primarily a visual medium, the words tend to back up or explain the pictures. This doesn't necessarily mean the pictures are *more important* than the words, but research shows people tend to remember what they've seen more easily than what they've heard. The point is, in tv the pictures explain a lot that the words don't have to. That's true in print ads, too. But print ads usually have one or, at the most, a couple of pictures, while a tv commercial has a series of them, divided into a series of individual scenes. And the scenes are further divided into close-ups, medium close-ups, establishing shots, zooms, tracking shots, long shots and the like. With all these pictures coming at the viewer at 24 frames a second, he or she cannot absorb a lot of complicated explanations from the sound track; nor does he or she need a great deal of explanation, since the pictures often tend to explain themselves. Therefore, as a general rule, the more the viewer is shown, the less you have to tell, and if you can show almost everything you have to tell almost nothing. For this reason many writers feel tv copy is a lot easier to write than print ads. From a strictly "writing" point of view that's true, but in a more basic sense, tv writing involves thinking up the concept for the commercial, and that's often as challenging, if not *more* challenging than writing the copy.

People speak and think in sentence fragments, not whole sentences. When we speak we begin sentences with the word "and"; we often end them with prepositions. That's the way many ads are written. Almost anything goes in ads, as long as it helps communication.

The main thing to remember about writing ad copy as opposed to the themes and book reports you wrote in school is that, much of the time what you read and wrote in school was written for a captive audience. As you know, the ad audience is anything but captive. You have to struggle to capture and hold their attention; anything that helps you accomplish that is good but anything that gets in the way, including the formal rules of grammar, is bad. Some of the best-written copy sounds loose, casual, off-hand. It's anything but that. In a philosophical or intellectual sense it may be simple and superficial but at its best it is tightly constructed, carefully honed, polished, commercial prose.

SUMMING UP

1. To begin with, write the copy for your ads as though you were writing a letter to a friend, telling him or her about the attributes or benefits of the product. Try to write the way you'd talk.

2. Copy the tone, pace and style of copy in ads in newspapers and magazines, or in award show annuals like *The One Show* book, which you happen to think are very good.

3. The first part of the copy is a sort of "bridge" between the headline and the main body of the copy. The middle part usually gives the details, facts, benefits and so forth. The last part of the copy winds things up. Sometimes it briefly sums up the product benefits and contains a so-called "call to action". Most writers like to end the copy with a clever last line that sums up what the ad is about.

4. With certain products, you might want the copy to sound somewhat aloof and formal. That's okay. But unless you want it to sound that way for a definite reason, it should have an informal, relaxed tone.

5. Try to avoid parenthetical phrases and complicated construction and punctuation—they tend to slow up things.

6. Tape record or videotape commercials. Transcribe the copy and study it.

7. Try to keep the copy for tv commercials to 68 words or less. Learn to write so you can tell a complete story within 30 seconds, which is the length of most tv spots.

8. Forget the rules of formal English, if they get in the way of what you are trying to communicate. In ads, language is a tool. Your job is to use language to sell products. Don't write crudely or punctuate incorrectly—if you do, your copy will sound sloppy and give the reader or viewer a poor impression of the product. But don't feel constricted by the use of formal English and grammar. Write and punctuate for dramatic effect.

NOTES

CHAPTER 11

HOW CAN YOU TELL WHAT WILL OR WON'T WORK?

You can't all the time. Neither can I. And neither can anybody else, no matter how rich or famous or successful an adperson he or she is. Advertising is partly art and partly science. It's partly logical and partly irrational. It's part fact and part fancy. It's a little like psychiatry or show business. It often works, but even experienced practitioners don't always know why or how.

People's moods and tastes change, opinion-makers come and go, scientific discoveries change the opinions, values and habits of vast masses of people almost overnight. What is in poor taste one season is all the rage the next; ideas that are revolutionary for one generation are old hat for the next.

The opinions of experienced writers and art directors are made up of intuition, judgment and plain common sense. Most of the time they're right, or at least not too far wrong. Most of them can spot a really awful or great ad immediately. But there's some work—some, moderately successful and some, in the long run, very successful—that is very difficult to judge correctly at first sight.

Bear this in mind when you show your portfolio to potential employers, including employment personnel who specialize in agency placement. Different people will respond favorably to different pieces of work.

However, as you show your portfolio to more and more people, you should begin to get a feeling about those ads and campaigns that seem to be going over well and those that aren't. What usually happens is that some ads are a smash with everybody, some seem to turn almost everybody off or confuse them, and most earn anything from a lukewarm to a very enthusiastic reception. Obviously, you should take out the losers and leave the winners. By pruning your book as you move from one interview to the next, you'll be improving it. Try to learn as much as you can about your portfolio from the people who are interviewing you. As long as your questions are diplomatic, you don't take up too much of their time, and you don't take criticism personally, most will be glad to help you. You are asking them for their opinion after all, and that's flattering.

If *you* have faith in a piece of work, don't be too quick to change it no matter what anybody says. You can be stubborn without being offensive about it. Listen carefully to what people tell you and agree to consider it. But consider it when you're alone—and do what you alone want to do. Wait until you have half a dozen opinions before removing an ad from your book. Always keep working on new ads and commercials while you're going through your round of interviews. You may be lucky and get a job in a matter of weeks, or it may take six months or a year or more. You may run into a whole string of helpful, sympathetic people or you may find yourself bouncing from one callous and indifferent creative director or group head to another.

You'll feel great when somebody tells you your portfolio is excellent and you'll feel lousy when they don't seem to go for it. Expect these swings of mood—all creative people are subject to them. Everyone likes acceptance and approval and all of us hate rejection and dislike criticism.

Also remember that what people tell you is only of value if it helps you get a job. In order to eat, you've got to work. Kind words and spiritual uplift will not buy coffee and donuts. Don't be lulled by people who compliment your work but forget to give you another person's name so you can have another interview which may lead to a job. Don't hesitate to ask them if they have a friend to whom you can show your portfolio. I have found that the most critical and demanding people often turn out to be the most helpful. I think of critical statements as tools I can use in order to sharpen my thinking. Be suspicious of people who fall head over heels for everything you've done. You're probably not that good. Ask each person you see which ad they think is the worst one in your book—no matter how much they like your work, there has to be a "worst" or at least a "least good" piece of work. If a couple of people pick the same ad or campaign, get rid of it.

SUMMING UP

1. Use interviews as tools—ads everybody likes should be left in your portfolio; ads almost everybody doesn't like should be removed.
2. Try to learn as much as you can about your portfolio from the people who interview you. Ask them for their candid opinions; most will be overly diplomatic, and that doesn't help you much.
3. If you are absolutely crazy about a piece of work that everybody else hates, leave it in your portfolio. They may well be wrong, although it's not likely. In any event, until it's clear to you why it's not good, you should stay with it; you must learn at your own pace. Nobody goes to sleep a rank beginner and wakes up a brilliant copywriter.

How Can You Tell What Will or Won't Work?

NOTES

CHAPTER 12

A CREATIVE CASE STUDY

Dick and John, a writer and art director, are given an assignment by the creative director. The agency is pitching a newspaper account. The newspaper, a well-known, highly-respected Long Island tabloid, wants to become a popular New York City paper as well. The client wants to sell his city version in competition with *The New York Times* and the *Daily News,* ten cents cheaper than the *News.* Dick and John confer at length with the agency president and the account executive in charge of the pitch. The current tv commercials, created by the client's former agency, have not worked. The paper has two celebrities under contract, one a former tv crime-show and minor movie star, the other a young New York Met baseball player. The four ad people agree the actor adds nothing to the paper's image and would not help establish any sort of personality for the paper. The baseball player as spokesman is a possibility, but Dick and John are uncomfortable with spokesmen for a product like a newspaper. Dick tells the president, "If you have a soft drink or some other product whose attributes can be described rather quickly, I can see using a celebrity to get attention. But a newspaper is a complex product, almost a living organism, with a distinct purpose, personality and tone, and I don't see a baseball player doing anything but trivializing the ideas and standards the paper represents.'' The account person is not so sure about the wisdom of writing off the athlete. Dick adds that he and John will keep an open mind.

The paper is an excellent product that has won eight Pulitzer prizes, two the previous year. Neither *The Times* nor the *News* won any. It has a larger local and sports reporting staff—100—than either the *Times* or the *News*. All four adpeople agree the paper should be positioned between the *Times* and the *News*. It would not be possible to convince New Yorkers anything is better or more complete than the *Times,* and the *News* is famous for it's fine sports coverage. But the two Pulitzers, and the larger local staff can provide backing for a claim that the prospective client's paper covers local news better than either of its competitors.

The four people agree the commercials should be inexpensive to produce, because the newspaper has only two million dollars to spend on media—a comparatively small sum for an assault on the home markets of the two famous competitors. The publisher has decided to try to get a foothold in the Borough of Queens—a stable, middle class area where most families turn to the *Daily News* for local information and watch the local tv news for everything else.

One problem the paper has is that native New York City inhabitants think it's a Long Island paper because of the many ads it contains for Long Island merchants. The president suggests conducting focus groups of *Daily News* readers to see if the agency can gather more useful information. Dick feels they have as much background as they need and the idea of focus groups is abandoned.

Dick and John have only a few days to come up with a campaign theme line and at least one thirty-second commercial. That night, they each do some work at home. The next morning, Dick brings in a rough commercial which involves the editor of the paper sitting in the newsroom talking directly to the camera. John has some wackier and more interesting ideas. One involves a talking horse, speaking from Acquaduct, a famous local racetrack. The horse, on camera, would move his lips, as though talking, a la the old *Mr. Ed* tv series. A voice-over ''horse's voice'' would talk about how well the client's paper covers sports, horse races and other local sporting events. Another of John's ideas involves the camera moving in on the Governor's mansion in Albany, New York while a Mario Cuomo-like voice-over talks to his relatives in Queens, supposedly on the phone, telling them how the client's paper is the only one that really keeps him in touch with New York City. John feels using Cuomo, or a Cuomo-look-alike, would be quite attention-getting and entertaining.

Dick feels John's horse idea is wrong. Privately, he thinks it's silly, but he doesn't say that. He suggests that the one thing any newspaper advertising must have is credibility and a sense of seriousness, and the horse, or any other idea so wacky, would be counter-productive, though he admits it would get attention.

John accepts that; it more or less confirms what he had suspected. Dick likes John's Mario Cuomo-idea very much, but wonders whether people in New York City will recognize the State Capitol Building in Albany. John suggests they super (words printed directly on the screen, over the scene the viewer is watching) "State Capitol, Albany" at the beginning of the commercial. Dick feels having an actor immitate Cuomo would be distracting. But he likes the simplicity of the idea of the camera moving in on the State Capitol while the viewer hears a voice-over. He asks John how he likes his editor-talking-to-camera spot. John thinks it's dull, but he tells Dick it's well-written, and suggests they keep it in mind. They move on.

Dick suggests secretaries talking to each other voice-over, while the camera moves in on the picture of the Capitol. The secretaries would presumably be Mario Cuomo's secretaries, complaining that "the boss" becomes angry when the client's paper doesn't come, and he has to rely on the *Times* and the *News* for local news. John likes the idea. Dick writes the script, shows it to John, then rewrites it three or four times, polishing it. It's not working. It's too long. He tries one of Cuomo's secretaries talking to her mother, down in Queens, a borough of New York City, on the phone. Then he tries a script in which the secretary is talking to her mother, and her mother is telling her the *Daily News* is good enough for her father and should be good enough for her boss. That implies that old fogies read the *News* and powerful hotshots read the client's paper, because it's more modern and up-to-date. Dick decides the script is getting too complicated and abandons the idea.

He still likes the commercial, although he feels some people may not understand what it's driving at. He rewrites it until he feels comfortable with it. He and John talk over Dick's suggested tag line, supered at the end of the spot—"Nobody, but nobody, gives New Yorkers New York, like the (client's paper's name)." John suggests they say "covers" New York, because he'd like to show the *News* and *Times* literally being "covered" by the client's papers. The camera would show the *News* and *Times* on screen and many issues of the client's paper would drop onto them in stacatto fashion until they cover them. The implication would be that the client's paper was overwhelming or "smothering" the two famous papers with its superior local coverage. Dick likes the idea and they agree to change the theme or tag line to "covers" New York City.

Dick has an idea for doing another voice-over. He suggests they use the publisher or editor of the paper, voice-over. The camera would pan down the client's empty newsroom, say at eleven at night, when the staff has gone home. It would move down and in on the hard-working editor talking to his wife. He'd be saying something on the phone like, "Sally, (his wife), your favorite editor's going to be a tv star! Yeah, they're using me in a commercial for the paper," etc. All of Dick and John's commercials use the same two references to 100 local reporters and two Pulitzer prizes. John likes Dick's idea but prefers the newsroom during the day, with a lot of staffers walking to and fro. He thinks it would be more interesting to watch. Dick says shooting the editor late at night would be moodier and more dramatic and would allow the viewer to focus his attention on the copy more easily. They discuss it further. Dick yields to John's judgment as an art director, that people walking back and forth in the newsroom would make more interesting tv. Dick is not convinced, but they are making progress, and have little time left, and he doesn't want to break the mood by arguing. Dick brings up his original idea about the editor talking to the camera. John thinks it's dull compared to this newest concept, and Dick agrees. John begins drawing tv frames while Dick polishes the copy, which he reads over and over again to John, to get his opinion of its flow.

The next day, Dick has another idea, for a commercial that opens on an empty newsroom. The copy would start with a voice-over of an announcer saying something like "If this newsroom was filled with all *The New York Times'* Pulitzer Prize winners from last year, this is what it would look like." Of course, it would be empty. The next frame would say something about the newsroom being filled with all the *Daily News'* local and sports reporters. It would look pretty full until, in the third frame, the client's local reporting staff marched into the newsroom, filling it to overflowing. Dick thinks this commercial would demonstrate the client's paper's superiority over both the others quite graphically. John likes the idea, but wonders if paying all those on-camera performers would be too expensive. Dick suggests they not worry about that at this point.

They struggle to make the middle frame of the commercial work.

Getting the reporters to walk on quickly enough might be a problem. They work on the exact wording of the commercial, to make it track perfectly with all the on-camera action.

Dick brings up his original commercial again. John suggests he keep the script "in his back pocket" when they show their work to the creative director. Realizing John thinks it's too dull to show to the boss, he drops it.

Dick writes a short rationale to explain the direction their work has taken. He used the word "cheap" in relation to the cost of the commercials. John suggests the word "inexpensive"; "cheap" has the wrong connotations. Dick agrees. They now have three commercials they like, along with a theme line and an execution of that theme line they think is highly dramatic and memorable.

They take their work to the creative director. He explains that the "state capitol" commercial cannot be used because implied endorsement of a commercial product by an elected official is illegal. It could be argued that no endorsement is implied, but the creative director has had experience with all the trouble that sort of approach can cause. He tells them it's just not worth the hassle.

He likes the editor in the newsroom and the "filling the newsroom" commercials very much. But he points out that the problem remains that most New Yorkers think of the paper as a Long Island paper. That point must be addressed directly. In his initial briefing, the president had made the point quite clearly, but as often happens during the creative process, it was forgotten. Dick and John are resistant to inserting a reference to the paper's Long Island's heritage. The three men talk about it. They rework the copy to include the reference, working at it until Dick is satisfied the copy is effective. They add a line to the tag line to the effect that "Long Island's great paper has come to New York." The "filling the newsroom" commercial is changed. It opens with a large, empty newsroom and a voice-over reference to "this is what a newsroom filled with all the *Daily News'* Pulitzer Prize winners would look like." The three men consider that a clever and intrusive opening. Then they cut to the same newsroom with *The New York Times'* relatively skimpy local and sports reporting staff. Since their staff is small, supposedly only ten or so, the point would be made ironically—and quite strongly. Then they cut to the client's paper's newsroom, with all their Pulitzer Prize winners and sports and local reporters. Of course, the room is full, making the point, which is made in voice-over copy, that the client's paper covers local New York better because "they have more good people" doing it. The creative director suggests they have the masthead of the newspaper visible in the newsroom throughout both commercials. Dick and John agree it would help identify the paper to viewers unfamiliar with it.

Later in the day, the creative director, Dick and John meet once more with the president and the account executive. They present their work, which is very well received.

That, in somewhat abbreviated form, is more or less how an art director-writer team might go about creating an advertising campaign. I have no idea how the scenario appears to a reader unacquainted with the ad business. I've left a lot of dramatic detail out for purposes of brevity and clarity. In reality, John smoked constantly, which drove Dick crazy. Dick kept getting interrupted with phone calls which irritated John, although John, good-natured chap that he was, said nothing. Dick, for his part, made no comment about John's smoking. For the previous six days, Dick had worked day and night to save one of the agency's other important clients. He needed a rest. John had just gone through a divorce and had to force himself to concentrate on his work. And so on.

Like two people alone at sea in a rowboat, Dick and John realize each needs the other. Each is quite confident and egotistical but each respects the other and will do everything he can to encourage his partner to use his imagination freely.

Whether dealing with each other, the account people, their boss or their bosses' boss, Dick and John strived to create an amiable atmosphere in which all participants felt encouraged to offer suggestions that would make the end product more effective. Creative people tend naturally to be protective of their work and resistant to any change. Whatever they feel, and however threatened they feel their work may be, they learn to project an attitude of accommodation and compromise. They develop a sense of timing. Instead of leaping to defend any suggested change in their work, they bear the fact in mind that, as time goes on, the other party may be convinced to change his mind or alter his view. They learn to walk the fine line between protecting their work and accommodating other members of the client-agency team who wish to contribute.

I suggest you reread the paragraphs which describe Dick and John's actual creative work. Notice how each of them builds an idea for a commercial, and indeed for an entire campaign, on the others' ideas and suggestions. It's almost as though their goal is to build a long flight of stairs, and each only knows how to build an even or odd-numbered step.

They get to the top by adding to and refining each other's ideas. Talented, fiesty people can go far in advertising. But those who go farthest and last longest, in my experience, are those who genuinely like working with other people, and have trained themselves to encourage other people to give the best of themselves.

For the sake of accuracy, I should add a brief epilogue to my "case history." The two creative people involved actually worked on a freelance basis for one of the smaller Manhattan agencies which was pitching the account. As it turned out, the information about the Long Island newspaper having a larger local and reporting staff than either the *Times* or the *Daily News* was inaccurate, so none of Dick and John's work was ultimately used.

The agency did not get the account.

SUMMING UP

1. To go farther and faster in the ad business, cultivate the art of helping those you work with get the most and the best out of themselves. Try to figure out things you can do and say that will make people enjoy working with you.

NOTES

CHAPTER 13

THE GUY WITH A MEDIOCRE PORTFOLIO MAY BE A PRINCE, BUT HE'LL LOOK LIKE A BUM

To repeat, your portfolio is a book or presentation case at least 11 × 14 inches that contains your sample ads and commercials, and your resume. Most portfolios are made of vinyl, with a zipper around the edge, and are filled with a dozen or 18 plastic sleeves, each with a piece of black paper inside, attached to the binding in loose leaf fashion. You simply slide each ad or storyboard between the black paper backing and the plastic sleeve and lo and behold, you have a "book" of your samples. It pays to get a portfolio with a handle, since that makes it easier to carry.

Let me clarify that you don't *have* to have a portfolio. People have gotten jobs carrying their samples in manila envelopes. But if you can afford a portfolio, it's best to have one. Your work is protected, it's a convenient way to carry material, and though you may come off as an especially cool and self-confident person by showing your jewels in very rough form, a portfolio will show people who interview you that you have some familiarity with the business.

Most professionals have their samples laminated in clear plastic. They carry these samples in a two or three inch wide hard carrying case which looks a bit like a large attache case. Laminating ads cost quite a bit, and when creative directors look through them, they often mix them up, so I wouldn't advise beginners to laminate their work.

What kind of samples should you have and how many? There is no specific number, but in round numbers: a half dozen to a dozen single ads for different products, and three or four campaigns each consisting of three ads with copy written for the first ad, would do nicely in most cases. Copy should be written for each of the individual ads. You can type the copy on the bottom of the layout, or in the space provided in the layout, if it will fit. You can type the copy on a separate piece of paper and place it beneath the ad, if your portfolio pages are big enough. Or you can put the layout (with the picture, headline and lines indicating where the copy should go) on one page, and the typed headline and copy on the facing page.

Broadly speaking, you can make ads for any product or service. You can write radio commercials. You can have single-page ads, double-page spreads, tv scripts or storyboards. How much is in your portfolio, and what form it takes are both important, but not nearly as important as is the quality of your work.

The kinds of products and services you pick to create ads for are very important. When I was in college, I used to do quite a bit of outdoor pistol shooting. I'd throw cans and bottles up in the air and try to hit them with my .22 before they hit the ground. More than half the solution to the problem lay in how I threw the objects in the air. If I threw them up right, I could usually hit them; if I didn't, I almost never could. The same is true of picking products for your sample book.

You want to pick the kinds of things that allow you to show off your talent to its best advantage. This means you want to avoid ad problems that are too easy and those that are too hard. Basically, no ad problem is easy, if your standards are as high as they should be. Each product or service involves a new, different and unique challenge. But there *are* clients whose products or services have little or no serious competition. While they're not exactly easy—in fact, most of them are very difficult to do well—the challenge they represent simply isn't that tough.

Charities, for instance. Ads encouraging people to give to charity aren't easy to do. Charities compete with each other for consumer dollars. But few charities face the kind of competition a toothpaste or cereal maker does. Nobody is *against* a cure for cancer, for example. Nobody *wants* people to get cerebral palsy or VD or lung disease.

One word of caution. What I've just said doesn't mean an impressive ad or campaign for a charity, a religious organization or a service such as one promoting the use of seat belts in cars equipped with them is not a good thing to have in a portfolio—*if it's a very, very good ad or campaign.* Specifically, I would say, if you have some good work along these lines, put it in, but don't fill your portfolio with it. A couple of good ads or a nice campaign for a charity or religious organization is enough.

What *should* you put in your portfolio?

Try to choose products for which you have some enthusiasm. Do you have a favorite brand of automobile? Are you interested in a sport? If so, create ads for sporting equipment or for a car.

Wander through a drugstore and buy a couple of packaged goods products—toothpaste, aspirin, shaving cream, cologne, sleeping pills—and read what *Consumer Reports* says about them. Create a couple of campaigns for each. Try some small space ads for a local merchant. If you have seen a good movie or read a good book lately, try some ads for them. Pick some products you know nothing about—tires, lawn mowers, knitting needles, bras, binoculars, cameras, sun glasses. Research them and write some ads based on your research. Try some ads for food—a soft drink, a cake mix. How about a detergent or a cleanser or a window cleaner? A room spray? A mouthwash? Take some ads from the pile of published ads you hate and redo them.

The basic rule for your portfolio is, a good ad is a good ad. But certain product categories provide almost insuperable obstacles for a beginner. Some products I've mentioned before fall into this category—banks, gasolines, brokerage houses, liquor. Obviously, it doesn't pay to spend a lot of time trying to build a portfolio of work for such clients. Women's cosmetics fall into the same category.

SUMMING UP

1. Most art supply stores have the kind of sample case you'll need to build your portfolio. They're plastic, about 17×22 inches or so, with a zipper around the edges, and clear plastic sleeves inside. You can buy additional plastic sleeves as you need them.

2. You can have your samples laminated in clear, stiff plastic. This helps protect them, but it's a very expensive process, which I wouldn't recommend for a beginner. Your work should be presented in a neat, orderly fashion, but it is the *substance* of what's in your portfolio, not the level of finished art and printing, which will eventually get you a job. Don't waste a lot of money on fancy type, pictures, etc.

3. An acceptable size for a portfolio would be: a dozen single ads (headline/layout in the plastic sleeve on the left, typewritten copy in the plastic sleeve on the right), and perhaps three or four campaigns, each consisting of three ads, with copy written for the first ad.

4. You can write ads for public service clients for your portfolio, but as a rule, it's better to create ads for products with serious competition. You can write ads for any kind of product; just make sure it's a real product. *Consumer Reports* gives you the facts about thousands of products. It can make you an 'instant expert' in any category in a matter of minutes. Try some ads or campaigns for "packaged goods" products—products that come in packages which people can buy in a supermarket or drugstore. Don't load your portfolio with ads for only one kind of product, even if that product category fascinates you. It's more impressive to demonstrate your skills on a variety of challenges. Don't hesitate to try some ads for local merchants.

NOTES

CHAPTER 14

HOW TO GET A JOB IN AN AGENCY CREATIVE DEPARTMENT

If you, or anybody you know, knows somebody who works either for an ad agency or one of their clients, by all means contact that person and see what he or she can do for you. Perhaps that person can get you an interview with an advertising or marketing manager at a client company, or better yet, with a group head or creative director with the agency.

If you don't have any important contacts you have to drum up some. It takes work, but it's not very hard or complicated. From the business section of your public library, get the issue of *Advertising Age* that lists ad agencies by order of billing. *Ad Age,* as it's known to most adpeople, is a weekly periodical. This particular issue is usually published some time in February. Hundreds of agencies are listed in groups according to the size of their reported billing. Reproduce on a copier the names of several hundred. Then get hold of the book I mentioned earlier, *The Standard Directory of Advertising Agencies,* or "Red Book". Agencies are listed in alphabetical order. The names of each shop's top management and its address are listed. By combining your lists, you can obtain the names and titles of the top creative people in each agency. Write to them, telling them you'd like a job writing ads and ask for an appointment within the next two or three weeks in order to show them samples of your work. A small percentage will answer. Most will tell you they're not hiring beginners, or aren't hiring any creative people at the moment, but some will tell you they'll be glad to look at your work anyway. Don't be discouraged. They tell almost everyone the same thing.

Call everyone who's willing to take a look at your work and make an appointment as soon as possible. Arrive early for your interviews and expect to wait up to an hour. Expect that some interviews will be cancelled or postponed when you call to confirm them the day or the morning before your appointment. Be patient. When an appointment goes as planned, remember, before you leave each office, to ask if there are any other writers or art directors the man or woman can recommend you see. If they like your work they will almost always recommend friends. By asking their friends for more friends to see, you can keep yourself busy interviewing for weeks or even months. Eventually, you should be able to land some kind of junior writing or art directing job.

I should mention that familiarity with a particular agency's work never hurts. If you come across a particular print or tv campaign you like, mention it to the creative director you write to, if his agency created it. Try to find out which ads have been created by the agency at which you have an interview. It will give you something to talk about during your interview.

What happens if you write one hundred and fifty letters and wind up with no interviews? It's not likely, but it could happen. Simply write another one hundred and fifty letters. Or call some of the people who didn't answer and in a polite way, try to find out why. Ask their secretaries if there is another writer or art director you may see. Keep at it. Be persistant. Don't be rude, crude or impatient.

A word about secretaries. Some will be extra helpful, but most of them are simply not interested in helping out anybody they don't know and who is obviously not important to their bosses. When you deal with one of them, keep your wits about you. If he or she appears to be putting you off, try to get his or her name. When you call the second time, address the secretary by name; the less anonymous, the more accessible he or she is likely to be.

If you don't plan to come to New York City to do your job searching, the procedures I've suggested should work just as well in another large city. A good idea would be to look up all the local ad agencies in the *Yellow Pages,* call and ask for the name of the creative director or president, and write to him. If you can, I'd suggest you come to New York City, because there are more agencies, more jobs and more experienced creative people there than anywhere else.

You may be offered a job in another department of an agency, perhaps the media department. The way to learn to make ads is to make ads under trained ad makers. Of course, you may need a job, any kind of job, and may feel working inside an agency is better than being outside. True enough. And perhaps you can worm your way into a low level job in the creative department once you're inside. Whether you want to try that or not is up to you. But it's better to try to get an actual writing job, even if what you're writing is pretty low level stuff. It is true that if you get a job in a small out-of-town agency, you'll probably wind up doing a number of jobs, including ad writing, client contacting, space buying, and so on. In this position, you can learn a lot about the ad business in a short period of time. And the fact that you've worked for an agency will help you get a job if and when you come to New York City.

It used to be a lot easier to get a job as a secretary in the creative department of a large agency and gradually move up to a junior writing job than it is today. But it still happens from time to time. If you do get a secretarial job, there's no reason why you can't do sample ads in your spare time. Try to show your work to some of the creative people when they have a free moment. Most will respond instinctively to the efforts of a hard-working beginner who wants to learn. If they like your work and think you're learning they may occasionally let you write some copy or may pass some small trade assignments on to you, and you'll be on your way.

SUMMING UP

1. If you have any important agency or client contacts, *use them.* Some beginners feel uncomfortable about "imposing upon" friends. Don't feel that way; it's the way things are done in the business world.

2. It's very easy to learn the names and addresses of advertising agencies around the country. An issue of *Advertising Age* which runs early in the year, usually around February, lists U.S. agencies, ranking them by the size of their billings. The *Standard Dictionary of Advertising Agencies,* better known as the "Red Book," available in most business libraries, lists agencies alphabetically. It provides names of senior management, addresses and telephone numbers. Using these two publications, you can learn the names, addresses and client lists of the largest U.S. agencies. If you want an interview, write to the president or creative director. Before an interview, look the agency up in the red book. The more you know about the person (and the agency) interviewing you, the more impressive you're likely to be.

NOTES

CHAPTER 15

HOW MUCH CAN YOU MAKE AND HOW LONG WILL IT TAKE?

The quickest way to start an argument in the ad business is to discuss salaries. Everybody has an opinion and very few people have any facts beyond those of their own immediate experience.

At this writing, New York agencies pay from $15–$20,000 to start. Most people seem to agree that within five to seven years a talented and ambitious person, especially one who's willing to change jobs frequently, should be able to make $35,000–$60,000 a year. Within seven to ten years, he or she should be able to earn from $45–$75,000. Within ten to fifteen years, from $45–$125,000 and after 15 years from $55,000–$200,000. Many people who start their own agencies retire rich.

I cannot emphasize too strongly that I'm printing these figures only to give you *a very rough idea* of the kind of money you can make, and the time it will take you to make it, in advertising at big New York agencies as this is written, in 1985. Perhaps one sixth of the creative people are on a very fast track, and will make a lot of money quite quickly. Perhaps another one/sixth will not make a tremendous amount of money. The remaining two-thirds will fall somewhere in the middle. It's the old bell-shaped curve in operation. It's very hard to come up with precise, immutable salary figures, because some people include profit sharing stock dividends and bonuses in their salaries and others do not.

My own accountant's firm handles the tax returns of nearly 4,000 art directors, writers and account executives, and several of the best-known New York ad headhunters and creative personnel chiefs are personal friends of mine. By interviewing both groups in confidence, and using no names, I was able to come up with figures I think are fairly reliable.

Personnel specialists ("headhunters" is what creative people in the business call them) explain that in addition to luck, "visibility" on key accounts in an agency is the key to higher salaries. Some people seem to have an instinct for words and actions that make them highly visible to clients and agency top management. Other, equally talented, if not more talented individuals, seem to fade into the woodwork at every opportunity. It usually takes these more passive people longer to climb the corporate ladder.

Generally speaking, it's possible to make more money faster by job hopping, at least for the first five years of your career. I'm not advocating you do that; the wear and tear on the psyche can be excessive. But it is generally true that the agency that gives you your first job continues to think of you as a junior writer or art director. The people who hired you can't bring themselves to believe the person they hired for $18,000 can be worth $35,000 or $40,000 three to five years later. (It's also true, of course, that if the right person takes a liking to you, becomes what is referred to in the trade as your "rabbi", you can move up very fast, especially if your rabbi is influential enough to assign you choice accounts). Of course, you can always try to get a job offer at another agency and use the leverage of that offer to pry more money from your present agency, but that's risky. If you're really sure of yourself, you can tell your present employer that you have an offer from another agency for a lot more money even though you don't, and hope he or she will try to match it. People sometimes do that when they feel they're not being rewarded amply enough. Sometimes they get raises and sometimes they get fired.

What kind of raises can you expect if you stay with the agency you started with? It's impossible to make a precise prediction but generally speaking, in Manhattan $2,000–$3,500 a year can be thought of as a fair but not great average annual raise, for relatively junior people. Promising creative people can earn raises of $3,500 to $5,000 a year. Of course, if the agency loses major clients and has a very bad year, raises will be lower or nonexistent. Now and then, you hear of fabulous raises—ten, and in one case, twenty thousand in six months' time. (In the latter case, a writer in his early thirties went from fourteen to twenty thousand in two years. Six months later, after receiving an offer of thirty-eight thousand from a competing agency, he was awarded forty-one thousand by his agency. This took place in the early to mid-Seventies, when forty thousand dollars was considered big money. As this is written, there are writers who jump from, say $28,000 at one agency to $50,000 at another. It's a fluke, but it does happen now and then.

Bonuses are awarded when business is good, although practices vary widely from agency to agency and there is no such thing as an automatic bonus. They can range anywhere from one hundred dollars to thirty-five or fifty thousand dollars at the end of a good year. I believe one, two, three weeks' or at the most a month's salary is most common. Bonuses after a particularly successful piece of work, such as helping land a major account, are sometimes awarded in the form of travel opportunities, agency stock and the like. In one case I know of, an art director who was already in the Far East shooting a commercial was told to take a month and travel the rest of the way around the world gratis before he came back. Sometimes people handling travel or airline accounts are given permission to make use of the client's services and the agency foots the bill.

Most larger agencies and perhaps most agencies of all sizes in New York provide employees with life and health insurance, profit sharing, stock options and bonuses of one sort or another.

Some agencies provide free cars for top executives, especially if they have a car account. All agencies with a worldwide network of offices pay moving costs and help their people sell their old homes and buy or lease new ones when they move from city to city or country to country. Most agencies provide employees with two weeks' vacation and after a number of years, three and eventually four weeks per year.

People have become rich from profit-sharing funds at certain large agencies. After twenty or twenty-five years, some are reported to have stashed away $750,000 or more. The maximum allowable annual profit-sharing percentage is 15% a year. In other words, 15% of a writer's or art director's salary is put into the agency's profit-sharing fund, and the money in that fund is invested in stocks and other ventures in order to earn interest. The way most of these plans work, employees have to work several years at the agency before they are fully "vested"; that is, before they're entitled to 100% of the money put away for them. One, two or three years, say, from the start of employment, an employee is made eligible for profit sharing, and he or she is then "vested" or awarded a certain percentage each year, until he is fully vested. In other words, after about five more years with the company, or seven, eight, or ten years in total, he or she is eligible to collect *all* due profit sharing upon leaving the company.

Plans vary, like everything else in advertising, and profit sharing depends, of course, on profits. Naturally, stock option plans are only valuable if the price of the stock is rising. Many agencies are still privately owned, and management can help make favored employees rich by awarding them stock which continues to appreciate every year.

SUMMING UP

1. As of this writing, most starting copywriting jobs in Manhattan pay from $15,000–$20,000, if you're lucky enough to land one. How much you make after that depends upon your talent, skill and luck. A *very rough guide* for Manhattan salaries, based upon the number of years you've been writing (as of 1985): 5–7 years, $35,000–$60,000; 7–10 years, $45–$75,000; 10–15 years, $45–$125,000; 15+ years, $55–$200,000.
2. Generally, there are slow-trackers, the people in the middle, and fast-trackers. The slow-trackers will make the lower, or left-hand figure in each case, the fast-trackers will tend to earn figures close to the right-hand side of each span. Perhaps two-thirds of the people will fall in the middle.
3. People who change jobs a lot tend to make more money quicker, but the wear and tear on your psyche can be brutal.
4. Most large agencies provide profit-sharing, bonus and stock-purchase plans of one sort or another. Long-term, the big money is in agency stocks; large blocks of stock are usually awarded only to top executives. Most profit-sharing plans, as of this writing, require you to be an employee from 7–10 years before you're fully vested. Well-run shops manage to put 15% of your salary per year into profit-sharing plans. They earn interest each year, and people who leave before they're fully vested contribute still more money into the plan.

NOTES

CHAPTER 16

THERE IS NO FREE LUNCH

Everything in life has its price. Ad making can be, and at its best is, great fun. Making ads involves traveling to interesting places, working with interesting, intelligent, talented people, meeting celebrities and making important decisions involving millions of dollars. It also involves frustrations.

By any standard, advertising is a very competitive business. Only by understanding that and understanding yourself and what you want out of life can you be sure you want to go into it. If you follow the advice I've given you in this book you're in for hundreds of hours of very hard work, and I can give you no assurances it will pay off. You will derive one benefit, though. You'll find out whether you love to make ads. If you do, you'll be able to put up with all the frustrations without letting them get you down. If, on the other hand, picking up a pencil day after day to write headlines seems like work, you'll know long before your portfolio is finished that the game just isn't worth the candle. In the long run, it's a lot less expensive to learn that lesson sooner rather than later. Ecclesiastes 9:10 says:

> Whatever your hand finds to do, do it with your might; for there is no work or thought or knowledge or wisdom in Shoel, to which you are going.

I believe that. I love to work hard, and so do my most successful friends. If my book helps you find and stick with something you love to do in life, whether or not it's advertising, it will have been worth the time I spent to write it and the money you spent to buy it.

SUMMING UP

1. If you discover you don't really *love* writing ads, try some other line of work. Advertising can be an extremely demanding and frustrating line of work, and if you don't get a tremendous kick out of the actual creation of the ads, there's no point in putting up with the rest of it.

NOTES

CHAPTER 17

HOW MUCH CAN YOU REALLY LEARN BY YOURSELF?

A hell of a lot, if you're willing to work hard. Helpful as it may be, this book is only a beginning. I can only provide you with the fundamentals of ad making. I can't take you by the hand and lead you to a job. (If that's what you want and need, the ad business is not for you.)

As I said earlier, the ideal way to learn to make ads is by working in an ad agency. The next best thing is to come to New York and take several of the fine evening copywriting courses offered by The School of Visual Arts.

I realize there are a lot of obstacles. But the basic attitude of the would be ad writer or art director must be, "I'm gonna do it come hell or high water". People in a position to help you admire that sort of spirit. They have little patience or tolerance for a passive, lackadaisical, won't-someone-come-along-and-help-little-old-me outlook.

If you can't draw, and you've never made a layout in your life, you can at least draw stick figures. If you can't type using ten fingers, type using two or four. My firm belief is if you are reasonably intelligent and can write a decent letter to a friend, you can land a creative advertising job, if you're willing to work at it long enough. You may not wind up one of New York's top ad craftspeople, but you can certainly hold down a decent job as a writer or art director. And maybe you *are* that one in a thousand really terrific ad maker.

SUMMING UP

1. Breaking into the advertising business as a copywriter is not a task for the faint-of-heart. You face great obstacles and many frustrations. But if you want to do it badly enough, you'll find a way. Management consultant Tom Peters has written, "There is no reality as such. There is only people's perception of reality." If your perception of the obstacles you face is that they're insurmountable, that's what they'll turn out to be. If your perception is that you're equal to the task no matter how hard it may be, *that* will turn out to be true. It's all up to you.

NOTES

CHAPTER 18

SOME POINTS TO PONDER

(1) If you have never drawn a layout in your life, try this for starters: take an ordinary 8 ½ X 11 typewriter page and draw a horizontal line across it, two thirds of the way down. The space above the line will be where your picture goes. Just under the line, you will print your headline. Beneath the headline, in two rows of neat horizontal parallel lines, indicate where the copy should be. In the lower right hand corner, leave room for the client's logotype.

You can make any kind of layout you want eventually, but start out using this simple layout at the beginning.

Don't start a headline at the top of the page, continue it in the middle, and end it at the bottom. Don't surprint it over the illustration. Don't print it on the bias. Print your headline in neat, block letters, so it's easy to read.

Your ad concept can involve showing several illustrations on one page. You can show a hundred small pictures, if you like. But bear one thing in mind: it's harder to read and understand a dozen pictures than one. The more complicated your visual element gets, the longer it's going to take to read and understand the ad. I usually suggest that beginning students stick to ads with one visual, or illustration, and a headline that runs on top or underneath the picture.

(2) If you just can't think of anything, draw a picture of the product and try writing a couple of dozen clever headlines that dramatize the benefit. Try being wise, witty, humorous, serious. Try headlines with a straightforward, editorial tone.

Write for an hour or more, then rest. Then try for another hour or so.

Try thinking of a situation that dramatizes the benefit the product offers or a situation that dramatizes what can happen to the consumer if he *doesn't* own or use the product. In other words, don't be afraid to try a negative approach.

Remember: *The essence of drama is conflict and contrast.* Charlie Chaplin said he always tried to make the pursuer in his comedies large and threatening and the victim small and frail. The contrast helped make his chases more dramatic.

(3) How long you spend on each assignment depends upon your own capacity. Forty-five minutes on and fifteen minutes off is a schedule that works for many people.

(4) Try to study the photos you see in ads. Try to make a judgment as to their dramatic value. Is the picture as dramatic as it could be? How could it have been made more dramatic? Could the lighting have been different? Look through photography magazines. Study the work of famous photographers. Try to get a feel for visual drama. Most students who have done a lot of writing but very little selling tend to try to *write* the consumer into a sale. They fail to value the persuasive power of pictures as much as they should. The more your pictures or illustrations tell the reader, the more enticing they are, the less work the words have to do.

(5) After you've come up with a headline you like, put it aside for a while. Pick it up a day later and see if it still works. If it's a little "blind" or indirect, don't worry about it. The key question, the only question really, is, does the headline/visual combination provoke the reader's curiosity?

(6) Try to view the product and the benefit it offers in a unique way. Don't be satisfied with a straightforward sales pitch. Try something wacky.

(7) If you're unsure of your headline's clarity, ask yourself if it answers this question in a dozen words or so: "I should buy this product

because...............?''. After reading your headline, and looking at the visual you, acting as the reader, should be able to answer that question in a few words.

(8) The way to involve the reader, to encourage him or her to participate in the ad is to leave a little something out. By that I mean, in order to entice or seduce him into reading your message, you have to be a bit subtle, a bit indirect. You must give some *hint* as to the benefit, without necessarily *spelling it out*. Benefits that are completely spelled out make dull ads.

This "leaving-something, but-not-too-much-out" business is a very difficult point to get across. In effect, your visual is "A" and your headline is "C". If the headline/visual is right, the combination of "A" and "C" will intrigue the reader himself into supplying the missing element, "B". He will be intrigued, or seduced or charmed into *participating* in the headline/visual combination . . . into *involving* himself in it. If you can get him to do that, he'll probably continue to read all the copy, or at least a couple of paragraphs.

Don't worry if this point is obscure. Eventually, as you become more skilled in handling combinations of words and pictures, you'll get the hang of what I'm talking about, and you'll begin to be able to do it yourself. Years ago, the people at Doyle, Dane Bernbach created an ad for the VW Beetle that showed the car and the one-word headline, "lemon." The reader saw what looked like a picture of a perfect car, which was being referred to as a "lemon"—in other words, a defective automobile. What did VW mean, the reader asked himself, by referring to one of his own cars, a seemingly perfect car at that, as a "lemon"? The reader's curiosity was aroused, and he read the ad.

(9) Does your headline and visual combination have *flair,* an unexpected quality, a fresh feeling, or does it just lie there like a dead fish? Is your writing, your choice of words and phrases lively? Is it active rather than passive? Study your favorite magazines. See if you can identify the differences between the way *Time* and *Newsweek* and *The New York Times Sunday Magazine* are written. Develop the skill of saying things simply, using short, active words and declarative sentences.

(10) Watch the Johnny Carson show. Study the way the comedians who perform deliver their lines. Study the way Carson delivers his opening monologue. Each word and phrase he uses, every arch of his eyebrow

and turn of his head does some work. There's very little wasted motion, few wasted words. That's the way your ads should work.

(11) Each ad should have only *one central idea;* it should attempt to dramatize *only one benefit.* An ad or commercial that talks about a number of benefits is like five people at once trying to give you directions to the nearest gas station.

(12) Don't worry if you have bad days. Ad making is a creative business. If great artists produce some mediocre work (and nearly all of them have), how much consistency can you expect from yourself, at the beginning?

(13) No matter how clever, provocative or wacky you try to make your ad, in the final analysis, it must deliver—however indirect or entertaining—*meaningful information* to the reader. Ads are not entertainment vehicles; they are sales vehicles. If you want someone to read your ad, you must promise and deliver a bit of *useful, beneficial information,* not necessarily in the headline/visual combination, but in the copy.

(14) If your training has been largely in fine arts, don't be intimidated by words. Words are nothing more than convenient substitutes for pictures. You may be just as good at slinging words around as any writer. Don't let the word people snow you—creating images with words is not necessarily harder than creating images with pictures.

(15) Get used to the fact that most of the ads you see published and printed in newspapers and magazines are really quite mediocre. Don't get the idea that since they're *real* ads they're necessarily *good* ads.

(16) Bear in mind there is no "right" length either for copy or headlines—just as there is no "right" number of visuals or pictures or illustrations to use in an ad.

(17) It should be clear by now that one of the greatest creative challenges, and one of the most fundamental, is to make an intangible benefit tangible and by using words and pictures, to make it come alive. How do you make something like "good taste" or "good smell" tangible to people who are not particularly interested in the product or its attributes in the first place? By learning to pack your ads and commer-

cials with ideas, languages, pictures and images that *evoke emotions.*
Beyond the staples, most of what we buy each day supplies emotional
rewards; the products and services we purchase make us feel better. Ads
and commercials must get the idea of the emotional reward across in a
fresh, innovative way.

(18) Generally speaking, headlines should be written in the second
person ("you") not the first ("I") or third ("he" or "she"). Putting
headlines in quotes is not usually a good idea. Quoted statements on the
printed page are more interesting in news stories than in ads.

(19) It is a good idea not to use exclamation points in headlines. If
you want vigor and excitement in your headline move the words around
until you achieve it. Exclamation points to indicate excitement are corny.

(20) It is generally a good idea to avoid using the elipsis (three dots)
in headlines. As in #19, try to move the words around so they do what
you want them to, instead of using symbols that can distract the reader.
I don't mean it's literally wrong to use either the elipsis or the exclamation point, it's just a heavy-handed technique. An ad headline that
contains either lacks finesse.

(21) If you've written a good headline that contains the name of the
product, see if you can write a better headline that leaves the name out.
Clients like to see their names in the headline, but consumers are interested in benefits, not product names.

(22) At the risk of repeating myself, I cannot emphasize strongly enough
that the one quality or characteristic that makes advertising effective is
emotion. Dramatic appeals to the emotions are behind almost all successful advertising. Even advertising that appears to appeal solely to
consumer's power to reason has an emotional overtone. Many consumers disparage the emotional motivations that influence their buying habits. They feel themselves above that sort of thing. But just because they
think they're unemotional, that doesn't mean they are. Emotions, after
all, are behind people's choice of a marriage partner, where they live,
who they work for, how they dress and so on. Usually, in advertising
an appeal to emotion must have strong overtones of rationality, because
most people like to think their important decisions are rational. Such
overtones can be integrated into an ad or commercial through the clever

use of art and set decoration, the tone of the copy, the vocabulary used to get the sales points across, and so on. If it's done well, the *implicit* message of the commercial, over and above the *explicit* message, will be: "this particular product, dear rational, intelligent, well-educated, careful consumer, is the one for you. It's the kind of product people like you should have in their home and have your name associated with."

Rational overtones don't mean ads or commercials have to look and sound like a page torn out of an encyclopedia. For nearly a generation, Doyle, Dane Bernbach created advertising for VW that quite artfully combined a lighthearted, witty tone with an underlying rational approach that is as snobby as any Cadillac or Rolls Royce ad. But VW's is *intellectual,* not class, snobbery and it's a lot more subtle than any Cadillac or Rolls Royce ad's snob appeal. The VW advertising, apparently for a "poor man's economy car," has created an image and personality for the vehicle that appeals primarily to affluent, well-educated, middle class, white collar and professional people. The proof is that the VW buyer profile has always included an unusually high percentage of upper income, college-educated buyers—buyers who, by and large, consider themselves above mere emotional appeal.

(23) Learning to create effective advertising is difficult because you have to train yourself to think both rationally and emotionally. Once you've decided on an approach, you have to "let yourself go" emotionally in order to tap your own unconscious creative reserve and make it work for you. It's the kind of mythic, primitive, symbolic process most of us are trained to avoid. Our schooling emphasizes the cognitive, not the passionate, approach to life. We are taught to steer clear of "emotional" and "impulsive" types. Business schools teach students to make "rational" rather than "emotional" decisions not realizing that many if not most business decisions are instinctive, creative decisions based as much on intuition as upon "facts."

The process that a creative person must learn to harness is the same one that holds sway over and heavily influences primitive cultures. Many of the myths, symbols and artistic traditions we regard as an inherent part of modern culture can be traced back to primitive rituals.

Artists are trained to make use of this unconscious/conscious process. But if they are lucky, artists are privileged to be able to work at their own pace. Adpeople, on the other hand, must learn to turn the creative process on and off practically at will. The demands of modern business will not wait long upon "creative inspiration". Time and tide wait for no muse. The client or the account people usually seem to want the work yesterday, last week or five hours ago.

(24) *Ads are more like stage plays than speeches. Plays dramatize a point of view; ads dramatize benefits.* Remember: we all do not always think, but we all feel, and we feel all the time. *Your ad must sink itself deeply into this world of feeling and you must tie the product benefit to it.* That, and that alone, is the key to successful ad making, whether in film or print.

(27) Read and reread the book of *Ecclesiastes*. It contains some of the most moving poetry ever written. Read *The Great Gatsby*. Study F. Scott Fitzgerald's use of language.

(28) If the thought of putting together an entire portfolio from scratch overwhelms you, try this approach; search through magazines for really awful ads. Gather a pile of perhaps fifty and redo them in your own way. When you put your portfolio together, put the "bad" ad on the left and your improved version on the right. Be sure to write copy for your ad. That kind of portfolio won't be as impressive as one you've made up completely on your own, but at least it's a start. And a slow start is better than no start at all.

(29) If you have trouble coming up with an ad, try to think of a situation that dramatizes the benefit offered by the product, or dramatizes the drawback of not having the benefit. Draw that situation and try to write a headline to it.

(30) I used to expect my SVA students to work from ten to twenty hours a week on their ads. It should take you hundreds of hours to put a decent portfolio together. Creativity and timetables do not mix. Do not set a time limit on your work. Sometimes an ad that looks good in October looks terrible in December. Ads need time to settle. After you've put a book together, put it aside. Then take a fresh look at it a month later. Be hard on yourself. If you don't think an ad is absolutely terrific, chuck it.

(31) To repeat: do not try to create speculative ads for products such as airlines, cosmetics, beer, soft drinks and whiskey. Try to make it eas-

ier on yourself by sticking to products with a specific and concrete benefit. Perhaps you can try to write a few ads for this book.

(32) Remember, if people see your portfolio, they expect to be able to understand and appreciate the ads without any explanation from you. It's natural for beginners to want to offer an explanation with each ad. Avoid it. Your work must stand on its own. Expect to sit silently, offering no explanations, when you have an interview. If the interviewer wants an explanation, offer it, but don't go overboard.

(33) I cannot repeat often enough that the headline/visual combination is the heart of the ad. If that combination tells, or at least begins to tell, or gives strong hints of telling a story . . . a story that dramatizes the product benefits, or dramatizes the harm that can occur if the person doesn't use the product, the ad will be successful.

Remember that word—"story." People like to read stories. Newspaper articles are stories. TV sitcoms are stories. Great written art involves stories. Magazines involve stories. The way people communicate with each other is to tell each other stories. Plays—whether by Neil Simon, Beckett, or Euripides—are all stories. In a very basic sense, your ad should be a short story about the product that people find inviting to read.

Very often, successful ad campaigns are concrete stories that dramatize abstract product benefits. Abstract headlines or headlines that refer to abstractions usually are neither interesting nor inviting to read. Visuals that are abstract, that don't begin to combine quickly with the headline to tell or begin to tell a simple story about the product or it's benefit, or the drawbacks of not having the product, are dull.

I realize that, in practice, this will be a difficult point to understand. Even in my School of Visual Arts night classes, it took my students weeks to get the feel of how this point applied to ads.

I'd suggest you study ads for abstract product benefits like taste in food ads, and strength and reliability in corporate ads. See if you can analyze why some ads work better than others. I think you will usually find it is because the ad maker used concrete elements—concrete statements, direct headlines, and pictures of specific things—to tell, or begin to tell, or begin to dramatize his product benefits.

One warning: don't use ''scrap'' for your visual. Scrap is any photograph torn out of a published magazine, book or newspaper that is used for some other purpose. Many beginners look for interesting scrap pictures and try to write ads around them. Fine photographs used as scrap may make your ad look prettier or more professional. But they foul up the creative process. You must learn to "see visually" if you are to be a successful ad writer. You must be able to imagine visuals that go together with your own words to form an impactful ad. Using somebody else's picture is like trying to borrow their insight and experience. Whether it's better than your own is irrelevant; since it's *not* your own, it cannot represent the unique creative contribution you, as an individual, have to offer an advertiser. It is the *idea* behind the word-picture combination that ad makers are looking for. Your *ideas* about advertising products with words and pictures are what will get you a job, not pasting some photographer's pictures in your portfolio to make ads that aren't completely yours.

Study the many corporate ads in well-known business magazines. Ask yourself how many of those companies you want to read about. Probably very few. As you study these dull ads, ask yourself, ". . . what's the story?" In other words, what is the tale this ad's visual and headline combination are trying to tell me? Is it a story I can understand quickly? Do I care to become involved in this story?

When you work on your own ads, and you think you've come up with a few successful ads, put them aside for a day or so. Then pick them up, or ask friends or relatives to read them, and ask yourself, ". . . what's the story? Is the story I have picked to tell about this product, using the headline/visual combination as my main eye-catcher, all that interesting?" Ask your friends and relatives the same question.

There is no such thing as an uninteresting company or product. If the company is sound and the product works, it's interesting to *somebody*. You can make up a story about that product or *any* product that strangers will want to read, if you are skillful enough.

(35) You may run into people, perhaps even some advertising people, who will tell you that you cannot learn to write ads from a book. Nearly twenty years of teaching copywriting to thousands of students has convinced me that is simply not true.

You *can* learn to write ads from a book that is carefully prepared, thoroughly researched and backed by years of experience answering students' questions about advertising and copywriting. I am not saying you can learn to write *brilliant* advertising within a matter of weeks or even months. As far as that goes, there is no substitute for on-the-job training by superb writers and art directors. But I am convinced there are literally thousands of young people across America who can *begin* to learn to write ads from a book.

Twenty years ago, with absolutely no experience in copywriting, knowing nothing about the agency business, I bought a book and created a portfolio. The book is out of print now, and in many respects it is dated. But by immersing myself in that book and writing and rewriting ads for months, I got myself a job. I was on my way. The job I landed wasn't a great job. My portfolio was no earth-shaker. But it showed a perspective employer I cared a great deal about ad writing and wanted very much to be a copywriter and was willing to give it everything I had.

We've all heard the story of the half full and half empty glass of water. Some people see life as a half empty glass, others see the glass in more optimistic terms, as half full. Most of my students who wanted jobs badly enough found copywriting jobs. It took some a year or longer. They found the going rough, even after attending two or three night courses at The School of Visual Arts. Other students landed jobs midway through the semester, largely because they were lucky.

Admittedly, only a small fraction of all the students I've taught became copywriters. They were not always the most talented students, judging by the work they showed in class. Many developed quite rapidly *after* they got a job. Although those who landed jobs were bright and hard working, what separated those who succeeded from those who gave up was not skill, but *determination.*

There is a lot people lack in their early twenties. But what you have more of, than you'll ever again have in your life, is *time* and *energy*. If you think you'd like to make your living writing ads, by all means, invest the time and energy it's going to take to get yourself a job writing copy. Keep your eyes open. Work on your portfolio. Do your best to give your employer a good day's work for a day's pay. Don't waste your energy competing with others—compete with yourself.

Remember, advertising *works!* And good advertising works a lot better than bad advertising. You'll get a great feeling of satisfaction knowing you're a very good copywriter, able to write very effective ads for clients. When clients and agencies come after you, and are willing to pay you a handsome salary to work for them, the inner satisfaction of knowing you're very good at your craft is a far more profound thrill than a fancy title.

I firmly believe the job market for young people consists of two markets; one for the optimists and one for the pessimists. One group of college students looks at the obstacles looming before them and decides they're impossible to overcome. Too much work is involved, too much risk, too much nerve, too much agony and sweat and struggle. Another group begins immediately to find ways over, through and around the obstacles. Their eyes are on their own distant goals. For them, job hunting is a series of opportunities. Lacking both the money and the opportunity to attend night classes at The School of Visual Arts, they learn as much as they can from a book. They put together a portfolio. Not a great portfolio, necessarily, but one that demonstrates two important things: that they've worked their tails off, and they love to write ads. Then, using that portfolio, they push and shove and plead and beg and write letters and take buses and drive and hitchhike—and finally, they get a job.

Some Points To Ponder

SUMMING UP

1. This chapter consists primarily of numbered points and is, in itself, a kind of summing up. One final bit of advice: if you think you want to make a living writing ads, *give it everything you've got.* The experience of going all-out cannot help but be a beneficial and valuable one for any young person. In this respect, whether or not you wind up as a copywriter is almost secondary.

NOTES

CHAPTER 19

LEARNING BY EXAMPLE

On the following pages, you'll find reproductions of a number of superb ads published during the past 35 years, along with my comments explaining exactly why each of them is so good. I selected these ads not only because many of them are classics and others particular favorites of mine, but because each illustrates one or more of the ad making principles or lessons I've been trying to get across.

All these ads are the result of a combination I wish we had more of in the advertising business: (1) two master craftsmen, working closely together, (2) knowledgeable, trustworthy, account executives who understood the difference between ordinary ads and great ads, (3) patient, gutsy, supportive, protective agency management, willing to give creative people the time they need to create great ads, and (4) a cooperative, trusting, gutsy, sophisticated client.

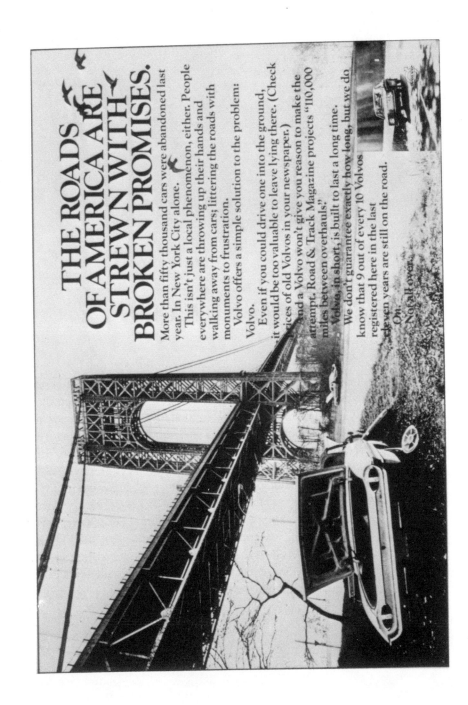

THE ROADS OF AMERICA ARE STREWN WITH BROKEN PROMISES.

More than fifty thousand cars were abandoned last year. In New York City alone.

This isn't just a local phenomenon, either. People everywhere are throwing up their hands and walking away from cars; littering the roads with monuments to frustration.

Volvo offers a simple solution to the problem: Volvo.

Even if you could drive one into the ground, it would be too valuable to leave lying there. (Check prices of old Volvos in your newspaper.)

And a Volvo won't give you reason to make the attempt. Road & Track Magazine projects "110,000 miles between overhauls."

Volvo, in short, is built to last a long time.

We don't guarantee exactly how long, but we do know that 9 out of every 10 Volvos registered here in the last eleven years are still on the road.

On.

Not all over.

114

Learning By Example

This ad, which ran some 15 years ago, is one of my favorites. It ran as a black and white ad, which made it look even more authentic and "gutsy". It looks very much like an editorial for better made, more durable cars. The ad characterized Volvos as better made cars, and used statistics to back up its claims. This ad and the one on the following page were among the first ads that made an association between a client's product and a controversial and timely "big idea", in this case, that Detroit made inferior cars that began falling apart as soon as the last installment was paid.

The series of ads caught the temper of the times and began building an image for Volvo that lasts to this day, and has made Volvo one of the best selling European cars in America.

Notice that you have to search hard to find a picture of the product in this ad. That's anathema to most car advertisers. It worked in this ad, because the ad itself almost seems to be more about the *idea* of longevity (like a newspaper feature article) than about the car itself. Plus, the small picture of the car somehow makes the ad's claims seem still more authentic. Also, it made the ad look different from all other car ads at the time.

Everything about the ad—the composition of the picture, its sense of graininess, its similarity to an editorial rather than an ad photograph, the ringing denunciation of the slick, sneaky habits of the big bad wolf competitors, the facts in the copy, the tough, terse way the copy is written—add to the impression of authenticity. In my view, this is one of the most powerful car ads ever written.

VW and Volvo were apparently the first to realize that the increasingly affluent American car buying public was better educated, more informed and more literate than any other buying public in history. They were actually hungry for information about certain products. These manufacturers and their ad agencies realized that these people, almost one-third of whom had gone to college and more than 10 percent of whom had graduated, could appreciate and would respond to fine writing and modern graphic techniques, and wanted to be talked to in more realistic, sophisticated terms.

The writers and art directors who worked on ads for these products realized instinctively that the implicit messages in an ad—the messages that were communicated non verbally, in a non-literal, symbolic way—were as important, and sometimes more important, than the explicit message.

IT SEEMS THE SUCKERS WANT AN EVEN BREAK.

The realization that the public does not like to be taken has taken a lot of manufacturers by surprise.

Toasters that suddenly won't toast suddenly won't be tolerated.

Nor will toys that break before noon on Christmas day. (We've been raising a whole generation of kids who think Santa's workmanship is terrible.)

People are showing their contempt for cars that break down on the way home from the showroom, too.

They're buying Volvos.

Volvos are built to last. Exactly how long, we don't guarantee. But we do know that 9 out of every 10 registered here in the last eleven years are still on the road.

If you buy a Volvo, you can keep it for a while, get out from under car payments and save some money.

We won't lure you into spending what you save on a New! New!

Volvo either. One Volvo body style ran 23 years without major change. To us, planned obsolescence has always been obsolete.

Volvo avoids the common practice of giving you as little for your money as possible. Example: We believe good brakes are a necessity. So we make power disc brakes standard on all four wheels instead of an option on just two.

Before other car makers even considered conventional seat belts, Volvo made three-point belts standard equipment. That was way back in 1959.

At Volvo, the new "consumerism" is nothing new. We were for it before anybody ever heard of it.

And if there is a sucker born every minute, you couldn't prove it by us.

They must be buying something else.

Learning By Example

This is another in the series of Volvo ads from the early seventies. (Another award-winning ad showed a derelect car, with the headline, "FAT CARS DIE YOUNG". It explained that, unlike most bloated, heavy "fat" American cars, Volvos were trim, well made and durable). Using the same techniques "Roads of America" used, in much the same way, this ad pointed out that people were turning to Volvos because they were fed up with cars that didn't last long enough and cost a lot to repair.

Incidently, an integral part of this campaign, repeated in practically every ad, was the claim, "Nine out of every ten Volvos registered here in the last 11 years are still on the road." That was true, but if you knew the facts, it wasn't all that impressive a statistic.

In the first six or seven of those eleven years, a comparatively small number of Volvos had been registered into the U.S. In other words, most Volvos registered in America in the last 11 years *were only a few years old.* The fact that a large percentage of a quite small total number of 11-year old Volvos, and eight, nine and ten-year old Volvos, was still running was not really all that big a deal, statistically speaking. Few people knew, in fact, that *eight point five* out of every ten of *all* domestic cars in America in the last 11 years were still on the road, and that *nine point two* out of every ten Plymouths registered in America in the last 11 years were still on the road. And there were *many millions* of those domestic cars sold—so of the 11-year total, there was a much higher percentage of old clunkers among them, still running, than there were of Volvos.

My point is not that Volvos weren't especially durable. Those made in the 14-year period before the early seventies, when the bodies and chassis were radically changed and they began to suffer overheating and electrical problems, certainly were. My point is that Plymouth and other domestic cars could have made exactly the same claim Volvo was making, since their durability statistics were even more impressive, but they didn't.

ELTON JOHN AT THE STEINWAY®

The Gibraltar of Rock.

In the music world today, there is a whole lot of shakin' goin' on.

And squarely in the middle of what's happening, you will find the Steinway piano.

The instrument you've always associated with great classical pianists has also become the mainstay of the important hard-rock and top-40 artists.

They specify it in recording studios.

They depend on it in concert.

Because among serious artists of every musical persuasion, there is a principal (we call it "Steinway's Law") which says: to make a lot of music, you've got to have a lot of piano.

For information about a lot of piano write to John H. Steinway, 109 West 57th Street, New York 10019.

Steinway & Sons

I'm willing to bet you've never seen an ad like this one for a fine piano. The basic idea of the ad is that Steinway is such a well-made, durable piano, even a "non classical" performer like Elton John, who beats hell out of his instruments, uses one.

The headline is, of course, a switch, or take-off or double entendre on the phrase, "Rock of Gibraltar". The "Rock," in this case, refers to the rock and roll of Elton John.

The shot of Elton John, obviously taken during a live performance, adds color and excitement to the ad. Most ads for expensive pianos tend to be sedate, rather dull affairs. The juxtaposition of a famous concert piano and a way-out rock star lends drama to the ad because of the unusual contrast depicted.

Notice the line in the copy, "to make a lot of music, you've got to have a lot of piano." That could have been the headline of this ad. But "The Gibraltar of Rock" is not only quicker and more clever, it's a lot faster. It packs the same kind of wallop the photograph does.

Usually, clients selling big ticket items want big pictures of that item in their ads. Their thinking is, if the customer is paying big bucks, he wants to see exactly what he's paying big bucks for. But in this case, the agency and the client had the guts to go with an extraordinary and very "unclassy" shot, which hardly shows the client's product at all. (I'm sure the word "Steinway" on the piano was retouched for clarity.)

I've spoken elsewhere about the importance of the element of "surprise" in your execution, and of the necessity of packing "news value" into your ad if its appropriate and lends itself to a provocative approach. This ad does both splendidly.

MAKE AMERICA A BETTER PLACE.

LEAVE THE COUNTRY.

Of all the ways America can grow, one way is by learning from others.

There are things you can learn in the Peace Corps you can't learn anywhere else.

You could start an irrigation program. And find that crabgrass and front lawns look a little ridiculous. When there isn't enough wheat to go around in Nepal.

You could be the outsider who helps bring a Jamaican fishing village to life, for the first time in three hundred years. And you could wonder if your country has outsiders enough. In Watts. In Detroit. In Appalachia. On its Indian reservations.

Last year, for the first time, Peace Corps alumni outnumbered Volunteers who are now out at work overseas.

By 1980, 200,000 Peace Corps alumni will be living their lives in every part of America.

There are those who think you can't change the world in the Peace Corps.

On the other hand, maybe it's not just what you do in the Peace Corps that counts.

But what you do when you get back.
The Peace Corps, Washington, D.C. 20525.

ADVERTISING CONTRIBUTED FOR THE PUBLIC GOOD

Learning By Example

This ad was published years ago. The ad takes a familiar icon—how many times have you seen pictures of the Statue of Liberty?—and gives it a slight twist, raising the Statue's arm, that makes the picture interesting.

The ironic tone of the ad was especially designed to appeal to the types of young people likely to join the Peace Corps in those days.

Imagine how many dull ways the creative team could have chosen to execute this premise. They could have played it straight; they could have shown starving people overseas and tried to write a headline about self-sacrifice. Many conventional ads of that kind work. But this approach accomplishes the same thing in a much fresher, more innovative way.

PIANO CHOICE OF SOLOISTS
SCHEDULED FOR THE 1972-73 CONCERT SEASON, BY ORCHESTRA.

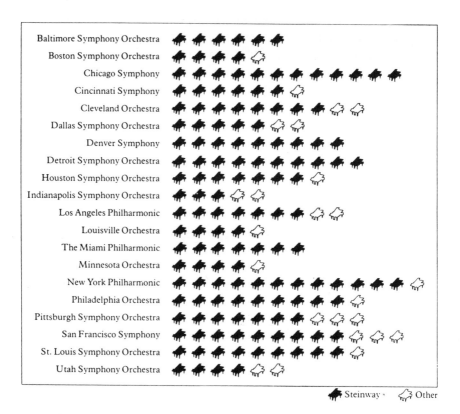

Steinway   Other

Steinway & Sons
109 W. 57 St., New York 10019

Learning By Example

This ad, which ran more than 10 years ago, has always been a favorite of mine. The point, of course, is that far more soloists choose Steinway pianos than any other brand. Unlike the Elton John ad, it's an extremely restrained, tasteful, understated ad. You have to study it a bit to understand the point it's making. But the graphic treatment, tasteful and clean as it is, invites you to read the ad and try to figure out what it's getting at.

The only "copy," as such, is way down at the lower right: "Steinway" and "Other". In its own way, the ad dismisses all Steinway's competitors as mere "others". It's as though they're so far below Steinway, they're not even worth identifying by brand name.

Notice this ad is signed "Steinway & Sons" at the bottom. There's no other logo, no identifying mark, no claim, no "reason why."

The power of the ad also comes from the fact that there are 139 Steinways and a mere 24 "others"—and the Steinways are solid black, to draw your eye, while the "others" are all white outline "lightweights".

Compare this ad with "The Gibraltar of Rock" on page 118. They both make the point that Steinway pianos are in a class by themselves. But they execute the message in totally different ways.

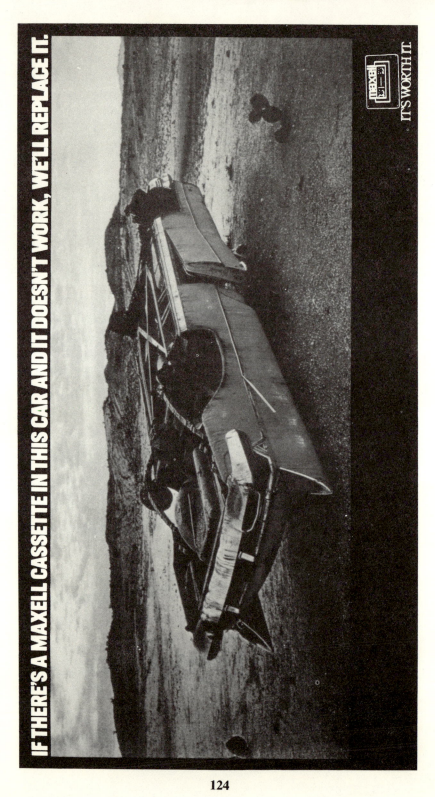

IF THERE'S A MAXELL CASSETTE IN THIS CAR AND IT DOESN'T WORK, WE'LL REPLACE IT.

maxell

IT'S WORTH IT.

124

Learning By Example

Posters are a lot like ads, except they have to work faster, since people have neither the time nor the opportunity to linger over them. They must attract the reader's attention instantly and deliver their message very quickly. For this reason, most posters depend quite heavily on their visual component. But it's a mistake to think of posters as mainly "visual."

In most cases, a poster is a virtual blueprint for the attention-getting power of the right headline/visual combination. The huge picture of the derelect car in this poster is a stopper. But it's only half the story. The first part of the headline implies there's a Maxell tape in this car. The "It" involves the reader in the picture in a particularly skillful way. He begins to wonder whether, in fact, there is a tape in the car—if, indeed, there is still a radio on the dashboard. The middle of the line "and it doesn't work" is still more involving. The reader is inclined to ask himself "what do they mean, *if* it doesn't work? Of course, it wouldn't work after years in the hot sun out there in the desert." But the thought is planted in the reader's head that it is at least *possible* that a Maxell tape, being as well-made as it is, may conceivably still work under those adverse conditions. Remember, they're not selling radios, but tapes. If there was a tape in that car, it might work well, even after years in the desert. The final kicker, "we'll replace it," delivers the benefit in a remarkably confident, almost arrogant way.

And the beauty of the whole thing is that this rather complicated and confident message about trust, reliability and durability is delivered in an extremely provocative way—*in seconds.*

"Maybe it will go away."

The five most dangerous words in the English language.

American Cancer Society

We want to cure cancer in your lifetime.

Learning By Example

This public service ad reminds people that they should be on the lookout for the danger signs of cancer.

One of the reasons the ad is inviting to read is because it appears to make few demands on the reader—there's no copy or almost no copy. That's great for a public service because, since there's usually no individual benefit a reader derives from such ads, they tend to ignore them.

By the way, my first impression when I read this ad was that it would have been an even better ad if the headline and copy were reversed. In other words, if the headline read, ''The five most dangerous words in the English language,'' and the copy, in much smaller type below, read, ''Maybe it will go away.''

Think about it. Which do you think is better?

Learning By Example

It's very hard to do terrific whiskey ads. Nearly all clients insist you show a big picture of the bottle, since customers in liquor stores tend to buy labels they've seen advertised, and tend to regard all others as "brand X".

Notice there are no beautiful people drinking the stuff, no swanky cocktail parties, no beautiful, slinky women. No cliches, in other words. Just a beautiful and very weird, fascinating bottle shot.

And the ironic, rather whimsical headline gives an especially unusual picture a whole new meaning. It adds connotations of status and class, but in a subtle, restrained and extremely powerful way.

These days, people are very concerned about conservation and recycling natural resources. Some years ago, it was fashionable to make lamps out of old wine bottles. This ad cleverly parodies both of those elements.

Notice none of the usual cliches—beautiful, slinky women in evening gowns at penthouse cocktail parties and the like—are used to establish and maintain a classy image for this expensive whiskey. Visual and verbal cliches tend to be dull and boring in adds.

The upscale reader tends to read this ad and react emotionally. In effect, the reader's inner voice says to him or herself, *this is the kind of whiskey which, if it were a person, would be a person like me—witty, affluent, urbane. It would be appropriate to stock it in my liquor cabinet and to be seen drinking this stuff . . . I think I'll try it.* In other words, the very powerful class-image communication that has occurred is largely *implicit. Explicitly,* all the ad says, in a cute, charming way, is that rich people drink this brand.

In New York, where Levy's was sold, most of it was consumed by Jewish people. The client wanted to expand the market. Great ads often have an *unexpected* quality about them. They come as a surprise to the reader, often because the visual and the headline either contrast with one another or because one imparts a surprisingly different or exaggerated meaning to the other. In this case, the line seems like a prosaic statement, until you see the visual. The Indian (and in some other ads, a black child or a Chinese person) is not only not Jewish, he's *so* not Jewish it's funny. It's hard not to smile when you see this ad. In a small but very important way, it has an enormous emotional impact upon the reader. And one of the most beautiful things about it is its simplicity.

The point of this ad is that using Olsten temporaries can be a better, cheaper way to get your work done than by hiring a huge staff. You have to pay life and health insurance and disability to that staff, and you don't have to do anything for temporary workers but pay the proper fee to Olsten.

You could dramatize that message many ways—perhaps by showing all the forms you'd avoid filling out when you hire temporary workers from Olsten. Perhaps you could write ads that talk about how carefully Olsten picks and chooses its workers.

This ad could have had a headline to the effect, ''Why pay for people you don't need?'' Clearly, this headline is a lot more arresting. Visually, the problem is that many of the appropriate visuals for this service are dull—people at typewriters, in offices, clerks at file cabinets, etc. So the creative team elected to do away with all that by creating an all-type ad with a magnificent headline.

The minute you finish eating your dinner dinner starts eating your teeth.

Unfortunately, not all the food you eat sticks to your ribs. Some sticks to your teeth. And the bacteria in your mouth change the sugar in those particles to acids that eat away at tooth enamel.

Your family can't stop eating. But they can brush with Crest after each meal. The fluoride in Crest makes kids' tooth enamel far more resistant to decay. Twenty-five years of tests prove how well brushing with Crest fights cavities.

It goes without saying that what applies to desserts at dinner applies to sweets at breakfast and lunch, too. And it applies even more to between-meal treats.

So make sure your kids brush with Crest after every meal. See the dentist every six months. And try to cut down on sweet treats.

We know of no better way to make sure that once you've finished dinner, dinner doesn't begin on you.

We're working to make cavities a thing of the past.

Learning By Example

This ad is effective because it contains a startling fact, presented in a straightforward, declarative style. Food, teeth and meals are very personal subjects. The benefits of flouridated toothpaste are very serious, important ones. It's not the sort of thing you can have much fun with— nor should you, when the facts are on your side.

I'm not suggesting you can't do clever ads for toothpaste. My point is merely that, when you do have a startling fact, it often pays to exploit it.

Bear in mind that Colgate and other flouridated toothpastes provided exactly the same type of benefits Crest did at the time this ad was written. Crest did not offer a unique benefit. Crest simply elected to dramatize their benefit, or to dramatize what might happen to you if you didn't brush with Crest, in a very provocative way.

This ad demonstrates quite clearly that you don't have to have a unique benefit to create provocative advertising. Sometimes, all you have to do to gain the lead on your competitior is to dramatize your benefit more effectively.

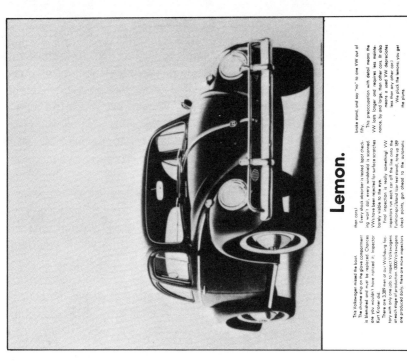

Lemon.

This Volkswagen missed the boat.

The chrome strip on the glove compartment is blemished and must be replaced. Chances are you wouldn't have noticed it; Inspector Kurt Kroner did.

There are 3,389 men at our Wolfsburg factory with only one job: to inspect Volkswagens at each stage of production. (3000 Volkswagens are produced daily; there are more inspectors than cars.)

Every shock absorber is tested (spot checking won't do), every windshield is scanned. VWs have been rejected for surface scratches barely visible to the eye.

Final inspection is really something! VW inspectors run each car off the line onto the Funktionsprüfstand (car test stand), tote up 189 check points, gun ahead to the automatic brake stand, and say "no" to one VW out of fifty.

This preoccupation with detail means the VW lasts longer and requires less maintenance, by and large, than other cars. (It also means a used VW depreciates less than any other car.)

We pluck the lemons; you get the plums.

Think small.

Ten years ago, the first Volkswagens were imported into the United States.

These strange little cars with their beetle shapes were almost unknown.

All they had to recommend them was 32 miles to the gallon (regular gas, regular driving), an aluminum air-cooled rear engine that would go 70 mph all day without strain, sensible size for a family and a sensible price tag too.

Beetles multiply; so do Volkswagens.

By 1954, VW was the best-selling imported car in America. It has held that rank each year since. In 1959, over 150,000 Volkswagens were sold, including 30,000 station wagons and trucks.

All they had to recommend them was 32 miles to the gallon (regular gas, regular driving), an aluminum air-cooled rear engine that would go 70 mph all day without strain, sensible size for a family and a sensible price tag too.

In fact, your VW may well be made with Pittsburgh steel stamped out on Chicago presses (even the power for the Volkswagen plant is supplied by coal from the U.S.A.)

As any VW owner will tell you, Volkswagen service is excellent and it is everywhere. Parts are plentiful; prices low. (A new fender, for example, is only $21.75.*) No small factor in Volkswagen's success.

Today, in the U.S.A. and 119 other countries, Volkswagens are sold faster than they can be made. Volkswagen has become the world's fifth largest automotive manufacturer by thinking small. More and more people are thinking the same.

*Suggested retail price.

Learning By Example

These ads are the progenitors of all the other great ads you've see in this book. It's hard to believe these ads were created nearly 35 years ago. To appreciate what an achievement they were, try to find some old *Life* magazines and *Fortune* magazines and study the ads that competed for the readers' attention with these ads.

I've spoken of the "lemon" ad elsewhere in this book. "Think small," a takeoff on the phrase "think big" was, and is a highly provocative phrase. The simple layouts were revolutionary. A small picture of the client's small car, surrounded by a sea of white space, was also revolutionary—and entirely appropriate to the product.

When these ads ran, nobody had ever seen, heard or read anything like them. Car ads in those days were big, glossy, dull, obvious and trite. Ads like these, and scores of other, equally accomplished ads created a personality for the VW Beetle while they explained precisely why it was such a good buy.

The *way* these ads explained the technical benefits the car offered—the way the headlines, visuals, type style and copy tone all worked together to create a personality for the car—is something you should examine very carefully.

Study current ads for foreign and domestic cars. Are any of them as good as these ads? Are they better or worse? Why? How could they be made better?

It's ugly, but it gets you there.

Learning By Example

When the U.S. landed men on the moon, every manufacturer who was even remotely connected with the event rushed into print with ads featuring their company's product. Every ad looked pretty much like every other ad. And nearly every ad was dull and boring.

VW took the opposite tack. It capitalized on the fact that the lunar landing module was aesthetically unappealing—actually, it was so ugly it was almost cute. The same thing was true of VW's. In effect, the ad was a reminder that VW's, although ugly, were dependable, just like the lunar module.

The only client identification was the VW logo. Here is another example of the remarkable power of taste and restraint. In contrast to most ads which tried to capitalize on the event, and which shouted and boasted in what appeared to be an arrogant and self-serving way, VW simply reminded people, in a gentle cultivated, witty manner that VW's are dependable.

The ad worked in the same subtle, charming, powerful way all VW ads worked in those days—to create and maintain a personality for the car that fit closely with the personality and socio-economic class of its potential buyers and the way they liked to characterize themselves and their life style.

"It was the only thing to do after the mule died."

Three years back, the Hinsleys of Dora, Missouri, had a tough decision to make.

To buy a new mule.

Or invest in a used bug.

They weighed the two possibilities.

First there was the problem of the bitter Ozark winters. Tough on a warm-blooded mule. Not so tough on an air-cooled VW.

Then, what about the eating habits of the two contenders? Hay vs. gasoline.

As Mr. Hinsley puts it: "I get over eighty miles out of a dollar's worth of gas and I get where I want to go a lot quicker."

Then there's the road leading to their cabin. Many a mule pulling a wagon and many a conventional automobile has spent many an hour stuck in the mud.

As for shelter, a mule needs a barn. A bug doesn't. "It just sets out there all day and the paint job looks near as good as the day we got it."

Finally, there was maintenance to think about. When a mule breaks down, there's only one thing to do: Shoot it.

But if and when their bug breaks down, the Hinsleys have a Volkswagen dealer only two gallons away.

140

Learning By Example

This is one of my favorite old VW ads. It's a perfect example of a headline/visual combination that, in a provocative manner, begins to tell a story relating to the product benefit. It's almost impossible to imagine a reader ignoring the ad.

The ad speaks of VW's reputation for quality and durability, of course. But it is the *way* it speaks of it that's important and unique. There's a down-home, laid back feeling about this ad and the way it communicates. Study the attitude of the people. They look like simple, honest, hard-working folk. There's almost something funny about them, but they're anything but laughable. You're charmed by them. And by the car. The implied message delivered by the choice of words in the headline, their relation to the picture, the simple type style, and the picture itself, is that this is a down-to-earth, solid, reliable, dependable car for down to earth, solid, reliable, dependable people.

In other words, this is more than a cute, charming ad. In a remarkably hard-hitting manner, it's delivering a very sound message about the car *and,* by implication, creating and maintaining a personality for the car. People feel their cars tell the world something about the owner. A car's personality must fit in with the kind of personality the owner likes to think he has, or that he would like to have other people believe he has. The "feeling tone" of this ad, skillfully created by the orchestration of all the graphic and verbal elements, conveys exactly the kind of impression about VW's that the client and agency wished.

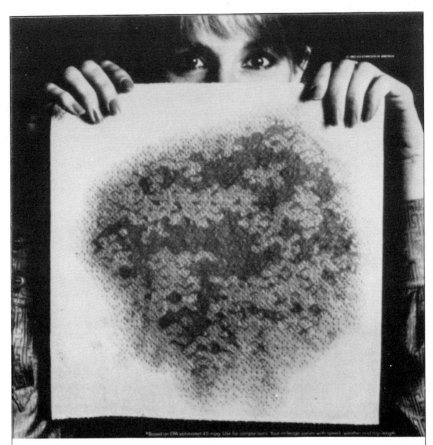

This paper towel contains enough fuel to run a Rabbit one half mile.

Astounding, isn't it?

But you probably think we're talking about some wildly advanced engine we put inside a Rabbit.

Perhaps an experiment?

Well, it's quite advanced: it's the Volkswagen Rabbit diesel.

And it makes the Rabbit the best mileage car in America.*

But it's hardly experimental.

Especially when you stop to consider the diesel's legendary reputation for durability.

Now the question is, do you really need the best mileage car in America?

Well, some people will tell you that fuel prices will continue to drop; that gas lines are a thing of the past.

Funny about those folks who made the same predictions in 1974 and again in 1979.

A lot of them now drive Rabbits.

Nothing else is a Volkswagen.

A remarkably vivid demonstration, in print, of the rather prosaic fact that Rabbits are very economical to run. One of the beauties of this ad is its simplicity—the simple way it says what it has to say, the way it's laid out, and the way the copy is written. Nothing gets in the way of, or detracts from, the message.

Many clients would insist that an ad for their car start with a big picture of their car. Both VW and Doyle, Dane Bernbach were much too sophisticated for that. If they had done that, this ad would look like every other ad for every other car. It doesn't. It looks like a VW ad. A very effective VW ad, uncluttered, simple and beautiful.

The ring that was heard after a five-alarm fire.

Jack A. Griesmar, Jr., an adjuster for a Cincinnati insurance company, was surveying the fire damage in a home when he noticed a fused piece of plastic on a table. It was so misshapen he didn't know what it was. But when he saw what was left of the dial, he realized he was looking at a telephone. A few minutes later, he was startled to hear the phone begin ringing.

Western Electric doesn't expect its phones to last through fires. But we're proud of the ruggedness built into the communications equipment we make for the Bell System. It's one of the reasons your telephone service is so reliable.

Western Electric
MANUFACTURING & SUPPLY UNIT OF THE BELL SYSTEM

Learning By Example

This message here is a simple one: Western Electric, the manufacturing arm of the Bell System at the time, makes an extremely durable product, a product you can depend upon through hell and high water.

This ad is based upon an actual incident. What's provocative about it is the big picture of a melted phone. It's hard to imagine anyone who's ever used a phone ignoring that picture. Since the photo is so compelling, the headline, by contrast, is quite straightforward. That's appropriate, because the ad is similiar to a news story.

Realizing they had an opportunity to create a powerful and compelling visual that was sure to attract the reader's eye, the writer and art director did exactly that. They did not slow down the communicative process with gory pictures of a burned house, or people in the background grieving over their lost possessions or any other cliches. In the background, barely visible, you can see some charred pieces of wood. They imply tragedy, danger and loss without picturing it literally. The art director and writer supplied the cues and let the reader participate in the ad by using his or her imagination.

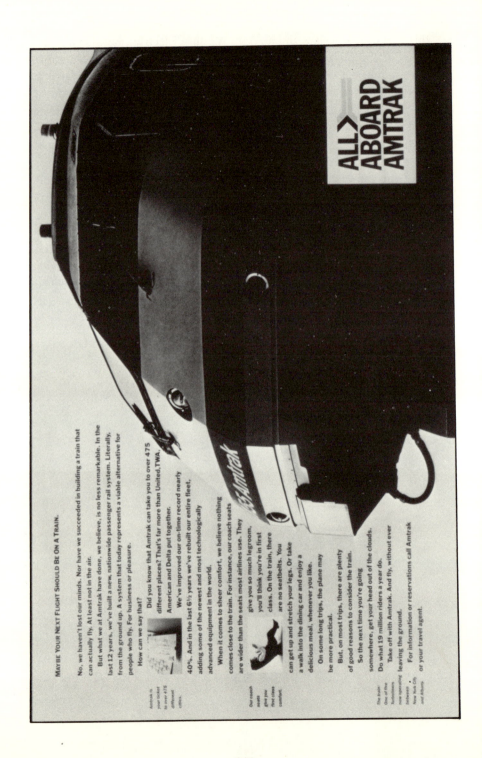

Learning By Example

This award-winning ad introduced the notion, novel at the time, that train travel could be as comfortable, convenient and pleasant, if not more so, than plane travel.

The headline is provocative, of course, because it associates the word "train" instead of "plane" with flight.

Notice the artful way the ad is laid out. The headline is set in a point size scarcely larger than the copy. It's arresting specifically because it breaks the "rule" that the headline should be set in much larger type than the copy. The massive shot of the magnificent looking train, as modern and sleek looking as any jet plane, is extremely compelling.

Small shots of certain features described in the copy stand in stark and dramatic contrast to the huge train. Most clients would want to feature large pictures of what customers get inside the train. The problem with lots of large pictures of smiling train customers being treated to good service and fine food aboard a train is that it would make the ads look like all the other dull, boring pictures of smiling passengers you see so often in travel ads.

Implicitly and explicitly, this ad delivers all the messages about the train that the client and agency believed were important—it's a modern, clean, comfortable, tasteful, exciting, speedy way to travel—indeed, in many cases, a better way to travel than airlines offer. But merely saying that would have been a flat and boring way to deliver the message. The clean, tasteful, provocatively laid out ad delivers those messages implicitly. Without giving it a great deal of thought, most readers tend to infer that clients with clean, neat, smart, tasteful ad headlines and layouts offer the public clean, neat, smart, tasteful products.

The one on the left has claimed more victims.

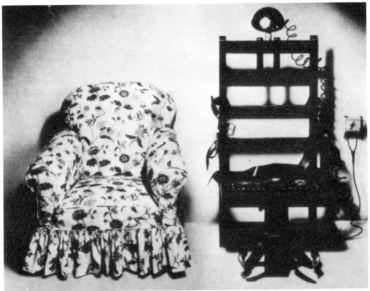

A nice, comfy floral-patterned armchair? What possible harm could that do to anybody?

According to the latest medical opinion, the answer is plenty.

The people at risk, we're told, are the retired (and nowadays that can mean mere youngsters of 55 or so).

They've worked hard all their lives. Now they feel they deserve to take things a bit easy.

Quite right, too.

The trouble begins when 'taking things easy' turns into lazing in an armchair all day.

Too many naps, too many snoozes, and the body can suddenly decide it's simply not worth waking up again.

The message from the doctors is loud and clear. Don't just sit there. Do something.

Opt for an active retirement, in other words.

You're always daydreaming about the things you wish you'd done with your life.

This will be your chance to do them.

Go ahead, build your ocean-going catamaran. Start up your vegetarian restaurant on Skye. Open that donkey sanctuary in Wales.

There'll be nothing to stop you.

Except money, of course.

And that is why you should be talking to Albany Life.

Not later on in your career. But right now, in your thirties or forties.

Start putting a regular sum into one of our high-growth savings plans and you can build yourself a very nice wodge of capital indeed.

We'll collect every penny of tax relief due to you. We'll then lump the two sums together and invest them on your behalf.

And our investment advice is arguably the best there is.

We retain the services of none other than Warburg Investment Management, a subsidiary of the merchant bank S. G. Warburg & Co. Ltd.

If you'd like to hear more about our retirement savings plans, post off the coupon.

We'd hate to see you sitting in a chair just because you couldn't afford to do anything else.

To learn more about our plans, send this coupon to Peter Kelly, Albany Life Assurance, FREEPOST, Potters Bar EN6 1BR.

Name

Address

Tel:

Name of your Life Assurance Broker, if any:

Albany Life

A startling and compelling headline, illustrated with a stark, simple, unadorned picture. Proof positive that, in almost every case, advertising is a much simpler combination of art and science than many agencies and most clients want to believe.

I think one reason this visual is so effective is because of the conflicting emotions each chair evokes. An electric chair is terrifying to look at and think about. An easy chair evokes warm, cozy feelings of safety and security. Juxtaposing the two, with no backgrounds and no people sitting in them, creates a remarkably intrusive image. Remember, the key elements of drama are conflict and contrast.

Learning By Example

The award-winning Nike ad series is, in effect, ads and posters all rolled into one. They're magnificent photographs on the one hand. They're celebrity endorsements on the other. They say a lot, without seeming to say much of anything. Most importantly, they work because they allow the reader, and in fact, invite the reader to involve him or herself in the situation. They're almost like a Rorschach test.

These ads work in much the same way as the famous Marlboro cowboy ads and posters work. They impart a virile, macho quality to the product, or rather, they encourage the reader to infer those qualities, without explicitly saying anything at all.

One of the few things on the Space Shuttle that didn't have a backup system.

Backup systems are essential to any manned space flight.

But space inside the shuttle is precious. How did the crew of the NASA Space Shuttle Columbia get a 35mm camera they could depend on, without having to take along a lot of 35mm cameras?

They took off with a Nikon.*

With good reason.

No Nikon has ever failed on a NASA space mission. In every manned mission into space since 1971, no Nikon has had structural damage from blast off. Or jammed.

Or had a mechanical problem. Or any problem that affected its performance.

A Nikon, as you may have gathered, is incredibly reliable.

So reliable it's the choice of more professional photographers than all other 35mm cameras combined.

There are four Nikon models designed for your special professional needs. The F3, the finest Nikon ever built for the professional photographer. The FE, a compact full-featured automatic. The FM which offers full manual control. And the

Nikonos IV-A—the world's only fully automatic 35mm underwater camera.

Whatever your needs as a professional, one thing is certain. Whether up in space, down on earth, or underwater, there's a Nikon to help take pictures that are out of this world.

Nikon
We take the world's greatest pictures.

*Camera used was a modified Nikon F. Future flights will use a modified F3 that has been customized with special wiring, lubrication and finish for use in space. © Nikon Inc., 1981. Garden City, New York 11530

Learning By Example

This is a fine example of a headline/visual combination that delivers an extremely powerful and convincing message almost instantly.

The reader's eye is drawn toward the center of the camera lens, framed with startling white gloves. Everything about this ad—the headline, the layout, a large picture of the product framed provocatively, the type set in blocks at the bottom to attract attention without detracting from the main visual and the headline set in huge type—is just about as good as it can be.

Learning By Example

One of the oldest, and some might say, dullest problems in advertising is, how to remind people in the Northeast in winter to fly Eastern to Miami. For years, Eastern has run ads and billboards and posters saying essentially the same thing.

This poster shows the usual bikini-clad beautiful woman—usually a ho-hum illustration. But it does have a number of advantages. It tells the reader what the ad is about, and it attracts male readers' attention. What makes the poster work so well is the headline's double entendre. The average person struggles desperately to use less oil in the winter. All winter long, his mind is on how much it's costing to heat his house . . . and how nice it would be to lie in the sun in Miami for a couple of weeks. Using "oil" to mean suntan oil and not heating oil, and showing a beautiful woman who has presumably just used oil that way, is a remarkably clever way to catch the reader's attention and draw it to the billboard's message.

Learning By Example

This ad is selling sightseeing in America in a rented car. It's an excellent example of how the art director and writer can work together to make the graphic treatment, or layout of the ad help attract the reader's attention and deliver the message.

Each of the small pictures, taken through a plane's window, pays off the headline. Study the captions under the first window. You'll get the idea immediately. But my guess is, knowing that the joke, in effect, will be repeated under each of the subsequent pictures, you'll find yourself reading the rest of the captions anyway.

The pictures are scattered throughout the copy, to help keep readers interested.

Study the copy. Like the copy in all the ads featured in this chapter, it's a pleasure to read.

LAST YEAR, A CAR OUT- PERFORMED 318 STOCKS ON THE NEW YORK STOCK EXCHANGE.

If you'd bought a new BMW 320i in the beginning of 1980, and sold it at the end, your investment would have retained 92.9% of its original value. If you'd done the same with any of 318 NYSE stocks, you'd have done less well. And you'd have forfeited an important daily dividend: The unfluctuating joy of driving one of the world's great performance sedans.

THE ULTIMATE DRIVING MACHINE.
BMW MUNICH GERMANY

158

Learning By Example

This ad is outstanding for what it doesn't contain, as much as for what it does. No pretty married couple draped over the hood, no lovely shots at sunset, no mansions in the background. All the cliches of car advertising are missing.

What you have instead is a simple, bold, provocative statement based upon a weird, wonderful fact the client or the agency dug up.

What the ad is saying is that a particular BMW, and by inference all BMW's have a very high resale value. The reference to the stock market is more than just a clever comparative. For BMW's, references to pricey things like stock market values is particularly appropriate—it helps maintain and support BMW's luxury image. There's an implicit message being sent here—that people who drive BMW's are also people who are involved with and interested in the stock market.

Also, the fact itself is startling enough to be very provocative. Notice also that there's no car pictured anywhere in the ad, only the BMW logo.

It should be obvious that what looks like a simple, startling, clever statement of fact is much more than that. It is a sophisticated piece of communication using a double meaning of the word "performed," which delivers a number of explicit and implicit messages about the product benefit to the consumer. All these messages have a common theme— luxury and quality—and all are delivered at the same time, in an integrated, organic way, almost a subtle way, in an ad that appears to be anything but subtle. While the ad appears to shout for attention, it also whispers, and both ways of communicating can be effective.

What's most amazing is that all the elements in this ad have been so perfectly orchestrated and blended into one, powerful piece of communication. It's almost as though the client paid for one ad and got a half dozen all wrapped up in one, all saying the same thing in a most provocative way.

Can you imagine a simpler, more provocative, quicker way to tell the reader that Farberware pots are backed by a long and distinguished history of quality and consumer acceptance?

Like the previous BMW ad, this ad is excellent partly because of what it does not contain. It does not contain trite, stereotypical pictures of smiling housewives and appreciative, smiling children. It does not contain pictures of kitchens or kitchen stoves. The only copy it does contain is the word "Farberware."

By implication, this ad says the Farberware company is a bold, self confident corporation, secure in the knowledge that its very name is synonymous with "fine quality" to generations of consumers. This ad is really an ad and a poster in one.

"I may be one of the few people in the world who has seen a canary given an enema."

So says the secretary to the remarkable, diminutive — five-foot-four, 100 pounds — Dr. Gus Eckstein (1890-1981), expert on animal behavior.

In an original article in the June Reader's Digest, Eckstein's secretary recounts her boss's work with birds, mice, cockroaches, etc. — and his magnetic personality that attracted such notables as Sinclair Lewis, Aldous Huxley, Thornton Wilder, Garson Kanin and Helen Hayes (who, walking into Eckstein's lab, had her mink coat attacked by frenzied canaries).

Eckstein "drew people to him by his intensity" — which is how The Digest" draws 39 million readers.

Learning By Example

I'm tempted to say, if you need a long, involved explanation of why this ad succeeds as brilliantly as it does, you shouldn't be in advertising.

But more seriously, this is an example of how words, properly treated graphically, can have enormous stopping power. Suppose this headline was set small. Would it have nearly the same effect? Suppose there was a picture of a researcher or a canary or an enema tube. They would detract from the whimsical, clever headline. Making the ad more explicit would be in poor taste, and would repel many readers.

The AR-XA Turntable.

It's a needle, not a knife that usually kills Carmen.

Learning By Example

This is a spec ad two creative people created for their portfolio. When it was written, nearly 20 years ago, the modestly priced AR turntable tracked at a mere one gram—far lower than most other turntables, even many expensive ones.

As you know, Carmen is stabbed to death at the end of the opera. The reference here was to the fact that most vinyl records of "Carmen" were ruined, or "killed" by styluses that track too heavily. Records on competing turntables, with heavy tracking forces, wore out much sooner than they did on an AR turntable.

The headline, of course, has reference to "the needle" (stylus) killing the record and "the knife" killing Carmen. It's cute and provocative because it mixes up, or contrasts the female with the record.

These days, most ads for stereo equipment feature dramatic shots of hi-tech equipment. The ads try to look as "technical" as possible. The last thing in the world most of these ads would feature would be a Blechman-like cartoon illustration, let alone a cartoon illustration of the turntable. The problem is that most ads featuring prominent shots of fancy-looking equipment tend to look alike.

The implication of this whimsical execution is that AR is so advanced and so confident, they don't have to resort to gimmicky, fancy-looking "hi-tech" pictures to convince the consumer of their value and technological achievement.

CHAPTER 20

SOME EXCELLENT PRODUCTS TO WRITE ADS ABOUT

EQUAL

It's a safe sugar substitute that leaves no bitter aftertaste and contains very few calories.

THE CASE FOR SUGAR

Sugar is not nearly as bad for you as most people think. An excellent article about the raw deal sugar has gotten in the press, and which contains all the background information you'll need for a pro-sugar campaign was published recently. You'll find it in the August, 1985 issue of *The Atlantic Monthly,* "Reports & Comments" section. It's called *Nutrition Sweetness and Health,* pp. 14–20, by Ellen Ruppel Shell.

THE NEW YORK TIMES

The *Times* is America's most respected, complete, authoritative and powerful newspaper and tastemaker.

AMANA REFRIGERATORS

In 1985, *Consumer Reports* rated them the best of all those tested.

Some Excellent Products To Write Ads About

SUB-ZERO REFRIGERATORS

In my neighborhood, these refrigerators cost $600 more than competing top-of-the-line models in the discount stores. They're not as deep as most refrigerators, so it's easier to get at things on the shelves. Much hand work goes into them. They're designed to accept removable exterior panels, so the front and sides can blend in nicely with a customized kitchen. Ask your local appliance dealer for information.

SONY CDP-302 COMPACT DISC PLAYER

Consumer Reports rates it at the top of all compact disc players tested, not because it plays discs better, but because it has more features than most of the others.

CABBAGE PATCH KIDS

The original Cabbage Patch Kids are hand-made soft sculpture dolls made in Cleveland, Georgia. They sell for $130 as of this writing. Each is different, has his or her own name and, according to the promotional material, is born in "Babyland General Hospital," a factory where everybody dresses up like a doctor or a nurse. Coleco, a toymaker, sells a smaller, less elaborate version for about $60.

YOUR FAVORITE ALBUM OR MOVIE OR BOOK

Write a campaign for your favorite music album. Currently, one of America's best-selling albums is *Born in the USA* by Bruce Springsteen. He has been the subject of *Time* and *Newsweek* cover stories.

BROWN GOLD COFFEE

Brown Gold is made with 100% Colombian beans, the richest and most expensive beans. Most regular coffees are made with mixtures of African beans, which are cheaper, more harsh and sometimes more bitter.

CRAYOLA

Crayola is the best-known brand of children's crayons. Perhaps you can write a campaign demonstrating all the fun a child can have with them.

Or how much cheaper and more durable they are than a lot of fancy, electronic toys.

SOHO NATURAL SODA

This is a new brand. There are ten flavors. No artificial ingredients are used in Soho. Twenty percent of the flavorings in the fruit flavors consists of natural fruit juice. The soda costs about fifty cents a bottle in stores and about $2 in Manhattan restaurants.

MADD (Mothers against drunk drivers)

Write a public service campaign to convince the public not to drink and drive. Bear in mind that the majority of "driving while intoxicated" accidents are due to young people having drunk too much beer at night and on weekends.

FORTUNE

Fortune is America's preeminent and most quoted business magazine. Study the magazine and see if you can capture its essence in your campaign.

RENT-A-WRECK

Rent-a-Wreck rents old cars at lower prices.

NEW YORK LOTTO

The New York Lottery (or any other lottery for that matter) offers participants millions of dollars in prizes. Remember that money is merely a convenient means of exchange; in and of itself, it means nothing. It is what you can buy, and the power, respect and admiration that money brings that you must try to dramatize.

FIT 'N TRIM

Fit N Trim is a low calorie dog food for fat dogs.

Some Excellent Products To Write Ads About

A CAVITY AND PLAQUE FIGHTING TOOTHPASTE

Several brands of toothpaste now contain both flouride and plaque fighters. Plaque is the hard film that builds up on teeth which are not brushed properly and frequently. Plaque buildup is the leading cause of gum disease and tooth loss in adults.

FROSTED MINI-WHEATS

According to *Consumer Reports* (October, 1986, p. 632) Kellog's Frosted Mini-Wheats is one of the most nutritious and best-tasting (i.e., sweetest) cold cereals a child, or an adult for that matter, can eat in the morning. The problem in selling nutritious foods is that almost nobody will buy them unless they like the taste. And it is next to impossible to convince children to eat a cereal that doesn't taste sweet. Although they're not as sweet as sugar-coated cereals, Frosted Mini-Wheats taste fine.

CHAPTER 21

ONCE YOU'VE GOT A PORTFOLIO, HERE'S A LIST OF AGENCIES YOU MIGHT SHOW IT TO

The following list of agencies in Atlanta, Chicago, Dallas, Houston, Los Angeles, New York, San Francisco and Toronto is the latest available as of November 1986. That means it's based on data from fall 1986.

The ad business changes rapidly. Agencies spring to life, merge with others and change letterheads and addresses relatively often, compared to ordinary corporations. The mergermania affecting corporations in general has affected the ad business to a large degree, especially among large New York shops.

So think of this list as helpful rather than gospel.

ATLANTA

Austin Kelly Advertising, Inc.
5901 C. Peachtree Rd.
404-396-6666

Bowes/Hanlon Advertising, Inc.
3925 Peachtree Rd.
404-261-1900

BDA/BBDO
3414 Peachtree Rd. NE
404-231-1700

Bozell & Jacobs Kenyon &
Eckhardt
3490 Piedmont Rd.
404-266-2221

Burton-Campbell, Inc.
100 Colony Sq.
404-881-8585

Cargill, Wilson & Acree, Inc.
3340 Peachtree Rd. NE
404-261-8700

Cole Henderson Drake, Inc.
3330 Peachtree Rd. NE
404-237-0057

Crumbley & Associates, Inc.
20 Marietta St. NW
404-577-7150

D'Arcy Masius Benton &
   Bowles, Inc.
400 Colony Sq. NE
404-892-8722

Evans, David W.
550 Pharr Rd. NE
404-261-7000

Fletcher/Mayo/Assoc., Inc.
5 Piedmont Ctr.,
404-261-0831

Green & Partners
100 Colony Sq.
404-874-8100

Kaiser Kuhn Bennett & Sharp
3400 Peachtree Rd. NE
404-233-5900

Liller Neal, Inc.
2700 Cumberland Pkwy.
404-432-7555

McCann-Erickson, Inc.
615 Peachtree Rd. NE
404-873-2321

McDonald & Little
400 Colony Sq.
404-881-8700

Ogilvy & Mather, Inc.
401 W. Peachtree Rd. NE
404-588-1866

Pringle Dixon Pringle
3340 Peachtree Rd. NE
404-261-9542

Rafshoon/Shivers/Vargas/Toplin
2 Northside 75
404-351-8212

Scali McCabe Sloves South
950 East Paces Ferry Rd.
404-233-7733

Smith Mc Neal Inc.
368 Ponce de Leon Ave.
404-892-3716

Thompson, J. Walter
2828 Tower Pl.
404-266-2828

Tucker Wayne & Co.
230 Peachtree St. NW
404-521-7600

CHICAGO

Abelson-Taylor, Inc.
360 N. Michigan Ave.
312-781-1700

Adcom, Inc.
479 Merchandise Mart Plz.
312-222-8900

Ayer, N.W., Inc.
111 E. Wacker Dr.
312-645-8800

BBDM
444 N. Michigan Ave.
312-644-9600

BBDO Chicago
410 Michigan Ave.
312-337-7860

Bently, Barnes & Lynn, Inc.
420 N. Wabash
312-467-9350

Beres, Lou & Assoc., Inc.
410 N. Michigan Ave.
312-670-0470

Bernstein, Ronald A. &
     Assoc., Inc.
875 N. Michigan Ave.
312-440-3700

Bozell & Jacobs Kenyon &
     Eckhardt
625 N. Michigan Ave.
312-266-2820

Brand Advertising, Inc.
400 N. Michigan Ave.
312-836-7777

Brody, David L.
6001 N. Clark St.
312-761-2735

Brown, E.H. Adv., Inc.
20 N. Wacker Dr.
312-372-9494

Burch Myers Cuttie, Inc.
22 E. Huron St.
312-642-0940

Buringame/Grossman, Inc.
35 E. Wacker Dr.
312-332-1515

Burnett, Leo
Prudential Plz.
312-565-5959

Burrell Adv., Inc.
625 N. Michigan Ave.
312-266-4600

Campbell-Mithun, Inc.
111 E. Wacker Dr.
312-565-3800

Christenson Barclay & Shaw
875 N. Michigan Ave.
312-943-1960

Clayton, Sidney Assocs.
711 W. Monroe St.
312-648-9500

Cohen & Greenbaum, Inc.
875 N. Michigan Ave.
312-787-2180

Columbian Adv., Inc.
201 E. Ohio
312-943-7600

Co-Ordination Group, The
640 LaSalle St.
312-648-5500

Corbett, Frank J.
211 E. Chicago Ave.
312-664-5310

Cramer-Krasselt/Chicago
333 N. Michigan Ave.
312-997-9600

Cramer/Krasselt/Direct
333 N. Michigan Ave.
312-997-9600

Creamer, Inc.
410 N. Michigan Ave.
312-222-4900

D'Arcy Masius Benton &
    Bowles, Inc.
200 E. Randolph
312-861-5000

DDB Needham
303 E. Wacker Dr.
312-861-0200

Dawson, Johns & Black, Inc.
500 N. Michigan Ave.
312-670-2200

Dimensional Marketing, Inc.
233 E. Erie
312-280-0700

Doremus Co.
500 N. Michigan Ave.
312-236-9132

Eiceff, A. & Co.
520 N. Michigan Ave.
312-944-2300

Eisaman, Johns & Laws, Inc.
333 N. Michigan Ave.
312-263-3474

Feldman, G. M.
444 N. Michigan Ave.
312-644-1800

Feldman, R. S. & Co.
676 St. Clair
312-642-4300

Fensholt, Inc.
180 N. Michigan Ave.
312-263-1132

Fisher Advertising
180 N. Michigan Ave.
312-236-6226

Flair Communications Agency,
Inc.
214 W. Erie St.
312-943-5959

Foote, Cone & Belding Adv.
401 N. Michigan Ave.
312-467-9200

Fortis Fortis Advertising
410 N. Michigan Ave.
312-329-1980

Frank, Clinton E. Adv., Inc.
120 S. Riverside Plz.
312-454-5500

Gardner, Stein & Frank, Inc.
20 N. Wacker Dr.
312-372-7020

Garfield Linn & Co.
875 N. Michigan Ave.
312-943-1900

Grant/Jacoby, Inc.
500 N. Michigan Ave.
312-664-2055

Grey-North, Inc.
Merchandise Mart
312-527-5030

HCM Advertising
1 East Wacker Dr.
312-329-1100

Haddon Advertising, Inc.
919 N. Michigan Ave.
312-943-6266

Hart Services, Inc.
101 N. Wacker Dr.
312-372-6300

Hill and Knowlton, Inc.
111 E. Wacker Dr.
312-565-1200

Huwen & Davies, Inc.
One N. Wacker Dr.
312-853-2860

Jordan/Tamraz/Caruso Adv.,
Inc.
625 N. Michigan Ave.
312-951-2000

Keroff & Rosenberg Adv., Inc.
444 N. Wabash
312-321-9000

Kebs & Brade Adv., Inc.
625 N. Michigan Ave.
312-944-3500

Kestman/Schmid & Assocs.,
Inc.
676 St. Clair
312-649-5800

Levy, Jack
225 N. Michigan Ave.
312-332-7540

Long, W. E.
309 W. Washington St.
312-726-4606

Mandabach & Simms, Inc.
20 N. Wacker Dr.
312-236-5333

Ad Agencies

Marcoa Direct Adv., Inc.
10 S. Riverside Plz.
312-454-0660

Marketing Support, Inc.
303 E. Wacker Dr.
312-565-0044

McKinney-Mid America
111 E. Wacker Dr.
312-644-3580

Meldrum & Fewsmith, Inc.
222 South Riverside Plaza
312-559-9100

Menaker & Wright, Inc.
645 N. Michigan Ave.
312-266-1177

Nader & Associates, Inc.
101 E. Ontario St.
312-943-9833

Nahfer, Frank C.
10 S. Riverside Plz.
312-845-5000

Niles, Fred A. Communications
1058 W. Washington
312-738-4181

OMAR
5525 N. Broadway
312-271-2720

Ogilvy & Mather, Inc.
200 E. Randolph Dr.
312-861-1166

Primer Advertising, Leonard,
Inc.
35 E. Wacker Dr.
312-263-5365

Proctor & Gardner Adv., Inc.
111 E. Wacker Dr.
312-644-7950

Rosenthal, Albert Jay & Co.
400 N. Michigan Ave.
312-337-8070

Schram Advertising Co., The
170 W. Washington
312-346-8585

Sieber & McIntyre, Inc.
625 N. Michigan Ave.
312-266-9200

Smith/Badofsky & Raffel, Inc.
444 N. Michigan Ave.
312-661-1500

Solk, Bud & Assoc., Inc.
875 N. Michigan Ave.
312-787-7055

State Advertising Agency, Inc.
36 S. State St.
312-855-2211

Stern Walters/Earle Ludgin, Inc.
150 E. Huron St.
312-642-4990

Stone & Adler, Inc.
150 N. Wacker Dr.
312-346-6100

Tatham Laird & Kudner
625 N. Michigan Ave.
312-337-4400

Tennant, Don Co., Inc.
500 N. Michigan Ave.
312-644-4600

Thompson, J. Walter
875 N. Michigan Ave.
312-951-4000

Volk, The John Co.
676 St. Clair
312-787-7117

Wardrop/Murtaugh/Temple &
    Frank
333 N. Michigan Ave.
312-236-2321

Weber Cohn & Riley, Inc.
444 N. Michigan Ave.
312-527-4260

Wells/Rich/Greene/Chicago, Inc.
111 E. Wacker Dr.
312-938-0900

Wilk & Brichta, Inc.
875 N. Michigan Ave.
312-280-2800

Young & Rubicam Chicago
111 E. Wacker Dr.
312-861-2615

Zechman & Assoc. Adv., Inc.
333 N. Michigan Ave.
312-346-0551

Zwiren & Wagner Advertising,
    Inc.
840 N. Michigan Ave.
312-280-8400

DALLAS

Bloom Agency, The
7701 N. Stemmons
214-638-8100

Carnegie Associates
5050 Querum Drive
214-386-5622

Case & Associates, Inc.
14305 Inwood
214-233-1080

Crume & Assoc., Inc.
1230 Riverbend Dr.
214-637-3746

Cunningham & Walsh Dallas,
    Inc.
4300 MacArthur Ave.
214-521-8700

DBG&H Unlimited, Inc.
1430 Empire Central
214-638-7723

Ezans/AFSC
4131 N. Central Expressway
214-521-6400

Keller Crescent
320 Decker Dr.
214-659-9220

McCann–Erickson
10830 N. Central Expwy.
214-361-1135

Point Communications
1700 S. Towers
214-744-1885

Popejoy & Fischel Adv. Agy.,
    Inc.
5151 Belt Line Rd.
214-233-8461

Reed/Melnichek/Gentry &
    Assoc.
7929 Brookriver Dr.
214-634-7337

Richards Group, The, Inc.
7557 Rambler Road
214-987-2700

Richards, Sullivan, Brock, Inc.
12700 Hillcrest Rd.
214-386-9077

Stern/Monroe Adv.
2905 Maple St.
214-698-1000

Tracy-Locke BBDO
Plz. Of the Americas
214-742-3131

Weekley & Assocs. Adv.
1545 W. Mockingbird
214-631-2535

Womak/Claypoole/Griffin Adv.
2997 LBJ Business Pk.
214-620-0300

HOUSTON

Bloom Business Agency
2900 North Loop West
713-956-6569

Bozell & Jacobs Kenyon &
    Eckhardt
1200 Smith St.
713-651-3114

Brown & Koby, Inc.
6601 Hillcroft
713-771-3855

Craig/Lamm/Hensley &
    Alderman Adv.
3100 Weslayan
713-621-2680

D'Arcy Masius Benton &
    Bowles, Inc.
2000 W. Loop So.
713-960-9070

Doner, W. B.
2900 Weslayan
713-871-9002

Eisaman, John & Laws, Inc.
2121 Sage Rd.
713-961-4355

First Marketing Group, Inc.
4669 Southwest Frwy
713-626-2500

Fogarty & Klein, Inc.
3303 Louisiana
713-528-3354

Goodwin Dannenbaum, Littman
   & Wingfeld
7676 Woodway
713-977-7676

Gulf State Adv. Agency, Inc.
8300 Bissonnet
713-776-9000

Ketchum Advertising/Houston
1900 W. Loop So. #1300
713-961-0998

Lowe Marschalk
3040 Post Oak Blvd.
713-840-0491

MDR, Inc.
800 Bering Dr.
713-972-1000

McCann-Erickson, Inc.
570 Post Oak Blvd.
713-965-0303

Ogilvy & Mather, Inc.
1 Allen Center
713-659-6688

Weekley & Penny, Inc.
3322 Richmond Ave.
713-529-4861

LOS ANGELES (BEVERLY HILLS)

Abert, Newhoff & Burr, Inc.
1900 Avenue of the Stars
213-552-2217

Admarketing, Inc.
1801 Century Park East
213-203-8400

Ash/LeDonne, Inc.
8222 W. Third St.
213-655-8222

Asher/Gould Advertising, Inc.
8383 Wilshire Blvd., Beverly
   Hills
213-658-7707

Ayer, N. W., Inc.
707 Wilshire Blvd.
213-621-1400

BBDO/West
10960 Wilshire Blvd.
213-479-3979

178

Baxter/Gurian & Mazzei, Inc.
Beverly Hills
213-657-5050

Bermudez & Associates
8200 Wilshire Blvd., Beverly
Hills
213-852-1011

Bertrand Advertising Agency
1680 N. Vine St., Hollywood
213-464-8181

Bozell & Jacobs Kenyon &
Eckhardt
12121 Wilshire Blvd.
213-442-2400

Brown, Keefe, Marine/Bowes
3435 Wilshire Blvd.
213-487-4600

Carlson/Liebowitz & Olshever,
Inc.
5670 Wilshire Blvd.
213-935-5571

Chiat/Day, Inc.
517 S. Olive St.
213-622-7454

Chickering/Howell
1900 Avenue of the Stars
213-277-9011

Cooke, Ralph K.
814 S. Westgate Ave.
213-879-5885

Cunningham, Root & Craig
Adv.
3600 Wilshire Blvd.
213-487-7575

Cunningham & Walsh, Inc.
One Century Plz.
213-556-1600

DDB Needham
5900 Wilshire Blvd.
213-937-5100

DJMC, Inc.
3435 Wilshire Blvd.
213-383-3332

Dailey & Assoc.
3055 Wilshire Blvd.
213-386-7823

D'Arcy Masius Benton &
Bowles, Inc.
3435 Wilshire Blvd.
213-385-0077

Della Femina, Travisano, Inc.
5900 Wilshire Blvd.
213-937-8540

Dentsu Corp. of America
3435 Wilshire Blvd.
213-931-8101

Diener-Hauser Bates & Co.
116 N. Robertson Blvd.
213-855-1900

Eisaman, Johns & Laws Adv.
6255 Sunset Blvd.
213-469-1234

Esty, KW.
9841 Airport Blvd.
213-776-5780

Evans/Weinberg Adv., Inc.
6380 Wilshire Blvd.
213-653-2300

Foote, Cone & Belding/Honig
2727 W. Sixth St.
213-736-8625

Forssberg, Hank
3275 Wilshire Blvd.
213-487-0671

Geisz & Rose Adv., Inc.
11110 Ohio Avenue
213-478-0251

Greenman Adv. Assoc., Inc.
307 S. 21 Avenue, Hollywood
305-929-2213

Grey Adv., Inc.
3435 Wilshire Blvd.
213-380-0530

Gumpertz/Bentley/Fried
5900 Wilshire Blvd.
213-931-6301

Hakuhodo Adv. America, Inc.
3250 Wilshire Blvd.
213-384-7979

Horlick Levin Hodges Adv.,
    Inc.
3780 Wilshire Blvd.
213-480-0708

Jensen & Ritchie Adv., Inc.
5670 Wilshire Blvd.
213-930-2600

Keye/Donna/Pearlstein
11080 Olympic Blvd.
213-477-0061

Kresser, Robbins & Assoc.
2049 Century Park E.
213-553-8254

Lewis/Coffin/Associates
801 N. La Brea Ave.
213-936-7212

Lorsch, Bob Company, The
3255 Wilshire Blvd.
213-386-2041

Mager, Kaump & Clark, Inc.
1777 Vine St., Hollywood
213-466-6251

Marsteller, Inc.
3333 Wilshire Blvd.
213-386-8600

McCann-Erickson, Inc.
6420 Wilshire Blvd.
213-655-9420

Michael-Sellers Advertising
5900 Wilshire Blvd.
213-937-2650

Ogilvy & Mather Direct
5757 Wilshire Blvd.
213-937-7900

Ogilvy & Mather, Inc.
5900 Wilshire Blvd.
213-937-7900

Pool Sarraille Adv.
357 S. Robertson Blvd., Beverly
    Hills
213-659-9753

Ramey Communications
3008 Wilshire Blvd.
213-384-2700

Reeds and Farris
2801 Cahuenga Blvd. W.
213-874-2801

Rogers, Weiss/Cole & Weber
2029 Century Park E.
213-879-7979

SSC&B, Inc.
5455 Wilshire Blvd.
213-931-1211

Scott Lancaster Mills ATHA
2049 Century Park E.
213-552-6050

Stern Walters/Earle Ludgin, Inc.
9911 Pico Blvd.
213-277-7550

Stursberg & Hewitt, Inc.
6671 Sunset Blvd.
213-462-6260

Swafford & Company Adv.
9908 Santa Monica Blvd., Bev-
    erly Hills
213-553-0611

Thompson, J. Walter
10100 Santa Monica Blvd.
213-553-8383

Wells, Rich, Greene/West
2029 Century Park E.
213-277-3200

Young & Rubicam
3435 Wilshire Blvd.
213-736-7400

NEW YORK CITY

AC&R Advertising, Inc.
16 E. 32nd St.
212-685-2500

A/M/S Advertising, Inc.
9 E. 40th St.
212-683-7030

The Ad Agency
251 W. 57th St.
212-581-2000

Adelante Adv., Inc.
386 Park Ave. S.
212-696-0855

Adforce, Inc.
235 E. 42nd St.
212-573-7200

Advertising to Women, Inc.
777 Third Ave.
212-688-4675

Albert Frand-Guenther Law
61 Broadway
212-248-5200

Alden Adv. Agency
535 Fifth Ave.
212-867-6400

Ally Gargano/MCA Advertising
    Ltd.
805 Third Ave.
212-688-5300

Altschiller Reitzfeld Solin
1700 Broadway
212-586-1400

Ammirati & Puris, Inc.
100 Fifth Ave.
212-206-0500

Ash/LeDonne, Inc.
1500 Broadway
212-221-0140

Avrett, Free & Ginsberg
800 Third Ave.
212-832-3800

Ayer N.W., Inc.
1345 Ave. of the Americas
212-708-5000

BBDO Direct
385 Madison Ave.
212-418-7200

BBDO International, Inc.
383 Madison Ave.
212-355-5800

Backer & Spielvogel, Inc.
11 W. 42nd St.
212-556-4984

Barnum Communications, Inc.
500 Fifth Ave.
212-221-7363

Barth, Frank
500 Fifth Ave.
212-398-0820

Bates, Ted
1515 Broadway
212-869-3131

Becker, Robert A.
90 Park Ave.
212-922-1000

Bergelt Advertising
605 Third Ave.
212-725-5588

Bergen/Stone & Partners, Inc.
666 Fifth Ave.
212-977-7474

Bisch, Damian
2 Dag Hammarskjold Plz.
212-355-1774

Bologna International, Inc.
149 Fifth Ave.
212-460-5980

Bozell & Jacobs Kenyon &
Eckhardt
40 W. 23rd St.
212-206-5000

Brouillard Communications
420 Lexington Ave.
212-210-8605

Burnett, Leo
950 Third Ave.
212-759-5959

Burson Marsteller
866 Third Ave.
212-752-6500

Butner, Lawrence Adv., Inc.
228 E. 45th St.
212-682-3200

CRK Advertising
1400 Broadway
212-575-7731

Cadwell Davis Savage/Adv.
625 Madison Ave.
212-350-1500

Calet Hirsch & Spector
135 W. 50th St.
212-489-7300

Campbell-Ewald of NY, Inc.
1345 Ave. of the Americas
212-489-6200

Cannon Adv. Associates, Inc.
444 Madison Ave.
212-759-8280

Cappiello & Chabrowe, Inc.
1700 Broadway
212-489-5272

Castor Spanish Int'l., Inc.
1450 Broadway
212-719-3808

Cato Johnson Inc.
100 Park Ave.
212-953-2650

Cavalieri & Kleier, Inc.
777 Third Ave.
212-758-7428

Chalk, Nissen, Hanft, Inc.
3 E. 54th St.
212-838-5900

Chenault Assocs., Inc.
605 Third Ave.
212-557-0600

Chiat/Day Adv., Inc.
79 Fifth Ave.
212-807-4000

Chin, Ted
825 Third Ave.
212-421-8989

Chislovsky/Fuhrman Assocs.,
Ltd.
444 Madison Ave.
212-758-2222

Clark Direct Marketing, Inc.
801 Second Ave.
212-661-9230

Clarke, George P.
122 E. 42nd St.
212-490-2212

Cohen & Marino, Inc.
315 Fifth Ave.
212-686-9730

Colarossi, Griswold
485 Lexington Ave.
212-490-0960

Comart Aniform
122 E. 42nd St.
212-867-7500

Compton Adv., Inc.
625 Madison Ave.
212-754-1100

Core, Chester Co., Inc.
515 Madison Ave.
212-759-6600

Crocker & Hull Adv., Inc.
20 E. 46th St.
212-697-7360

Cunningham & Walsh, Inc.
260 Madison Ave.
212-683-4900

DDB Group Two, Inc.
444 Madison Ave.
212-826-0200

DDB Needham
437 Madison Ave.
212-415-2000

DFS Dorland
405 Lexington Ave.
212-661-0800

DYR, Inc.
1114 Ave. of the Americas
212-869-8350

D'Arcy Masius Benton &
    Bowles, Inc.
909 Third Ave.
212-758-6200

De Krig Advertising
270 Madison Ave.
212-532-3260

Della Femina, Travisano
212-421-7180

Deutsch, David
655 Third Ave.
212-867-0044

Deutsch, Shea & Evans, Inc.
49 E. 53rd St.
212-688-0500

Diener/Hauser/Bates Co.
25 W. 43rd St.
212-840-3300

Dilorio, Wergeles, Inc.
420 Lexington Ave.
212-986-7850

Donino Pace, Inc.
275 Madison Ave.
212-696-5760

Doremus & Co.
120 Broadway
212-964-0700

Dorritie & Lyons, Inc.
655 Third Ave.
212-687-9394

Drossman/Lehmann/Marino/
    Reveley, Inc.
105 Madison Ave.
212-683-0888

Eicoff, A. & Co.
675 Third Ave.
212-883-9500

Eisaman, Johns & Laws, Inc.
488 Madison Ave.
212-838-8570

Eisenman & Enock, Inc.
25 Hudson St.
212-431-1000

Emmerling, John
135 E. 55th St.
212-751-7460

Epstein/Raboy Adv., Inc.
800 Third Ave.
212-688-4000

Esty, William
100 E. 42nd St.
212-697-1600

Fairfax, Inc.
635 Madison Ave.
212-350-1800

Fearon/O'Leary/Kaprielian
1995 Broadway
212-580-9494

Ferber/Janklow/Chimbel/Bender,
    Inc.
1790 Broadway
212-581-6760

Firestone and Associates
1345 Ave. of the Americas
212-247-4900

Fisher/Feld
888 Seventh Ave.
212-246-3900

Fisher Jackson Levy Flaxman
    Inc.
729 Seventh Ave.
212-246-3900

Fones & Mann, Inc.
200 Madison Ave.
212-689-9870

Font & Vaamonde Assocs., Inc.
183 Madison Ave.
212-679-9170

The Food Group
169 Lexington Ave.
212-725-5766

Foote, Cone & Belding, Inc.
101 Park Ave.
212-907-1000

Furman, Roth Advertising
1700 Broadway
212-757-7393

GGK New York
1515 Broadway
212-840-1250

G.M. Communications
240 E. 56th St.
212-593-3088

Gallagher Group, Inc.
1250 Broadway
212-563-3611

Gamut-Mitchell, Inc.
390 Fifth Ave.
212-596-1800

Gaynor Falcone & Assocs.
133 E. 58th St.
212-688-6900

Geer, Du Bois, Inc.
114 Fifth Ave.
212-741-1900

Geers Gross
220 E. 42nd St.
212-916-8000

Glasheen Adv., Inc.
300 E. 34th St.
212-889-3188

Gleckler & Spiegel
605 Third Ave.
212-867-3930

Graber & Cohen Inc.
Advertising
3 E. 54th St.
212-421-5200

Grant, M.I.
470 Park Avenue S.
212-679-9100

Great Scott Advertising Co.,
Inc.
57 W. 57th St.
212-826-2050

Greene & Claire, Inc.
10 W. 33rd St.
212-695-5800

Greengage Assoc., Inc.
747 Third Ave.
212-752-8866

Grey Adv., Inc.
777 Third Ave.
212-546-2000

Grey & Davis, Inc.
777 Third Ave.
212-546-2200

Grey Direct
777 Third Ave.
212-546-1800

Grey Lyon & King
405 Lexington Ave.
212-490-1361

Grey Medical Adv., Inc. (Affl.)
800 Third Ave.
212-752-2600

Griffin Bacal, Inc.
380 Lexington Ave.
212-687-2500

Gross Townsend Frank, Inc.
149 Fifth Ave.
212-475-4040

HBM/Creamer Inc.
1633 Broadway
212-887-8000

HBM Stiefel Adv., Inc.
405 Lexington Ave.
212-889-1900

Hall Decker McKibbin, Inc.
228 E. 45th St.
212-752-9170

Hall/Haerr/Peterson & Harney,
    Inc.
331 Madison Ave.
212-867-6633

Hammond Farrell, Inc.
105 Madison Ave.
212-696-5710

Hansen/Nigro & Wulfhorst, Inc.
205 Lexington Ave.
212-889-1540

Hanson, Fasler & Assocs., Inc.
19 W. 44th St.
212-840-3890

Harrison/Higgins, Inc.
71 Vanderbilt Ave.
212-557-2650

Henderson Friedlich Graf &
    Doyle, Inc.
600 Third Ave.
212-687-2300

Herman & Rosner Enterprises
110 E. 59th St.
212-355-3560

Hicks & Greist, Inc.
220 E. 42nd St.
212-370-9600

Hodes, Bernard Advertising
555 Madison Ave.
212-758-2600

Holland & Callaway, Inc.
767 Third Ave.
212-308-2750

Homer & Durham Adv., Ltd.
485 Lexington Ave.
212-370-9700

Intermarco Advertising
4 W. 58th St.
212-980-8550

Isidore Lefkowitz Elgert, Inc.
625 Madison Ave.
212-826-3400

Itta, John Paul, Inc.
680 Fifth Ave.
212-541-4460

Jameson Adv., Inc.
750 Third Ave.
212-867-2323

Jarman, Spitzer & Felix, Inc.
205 E. 42nd St.
212-661-3322

Johns, William B. & Partners,
    Ltd.
425 E. 61st St.
212-753-1690

Johnston, Jim Advertising, Inc.
551 Fifth Ave.
212-490-2121

Jordan, Manning, Case, Taylor
    & McGrath, Inc.
445 Park Ave.
212-326-9100

Kallir, Philips, Ross, Inc.
605 Third Ave.
212-878-3700

Ketchum Advertising
1133 Ave. of the Americas
212-536-8800

Klemtner Adv., Inc.
625 Madison Ave.
212-350-0400

Kolker, Talley, Hermann
171 Madison Ave.
212-889-7200

Kolody, John F.
22 E. 49th St.
212-935-5353

Korey, Kay & Partners
130 Fifth Ave.
212-620-4300

Koreyikay & Partners
15 E. 75th St.
212-744-1166

Kornhauser & Calene, Inc.
228 E. 45th St.
212-684-6700

Launey/Hachman & Harris, Inc.
292 Madison Ave.
212-355-4100

Laurence, Charles & Free, Inc.
261 Madison Ave.
212-661-0200

Lavey, Wolff, Swift, Inc.
488 Madison Ave.
212-593-3630

Leber Katz Partners, Inc.
767 Fifth Ave.
212-705-1000

Lefton, Al Paul
71 Vanderbilt Ave.
212-867-5100

Levine/Huntley/Schmidt &
    Beaver, Inc.
250 Park Ave.
212-557-0900

Lweandowski Enterprises, Inc.
454 W. 46th St.
212-757-7005

Lipman Adv. Co.
185 Madison Ave.
212-684-1100

Lockhart & Pettus, Inc.
60 E. 42nd St.
212-922-1670

Lois Pitts Gershon, Inc.
650 Fifth Ave.
212-974-1400

Lord/Geller/Frederico/Einstein
655 Madison Ave.
212-421-6050

MCA Advertising, Inc.
405 Lexington Ave.
212-661-5491

MMSM Advertising
555 Madison Ave.
212-832-3750

Mahoney & Assoc., H.E., Inc.
301 W. 53rd St.
212-664-1066

Mandabach & Simms, Inc.
801 Second Ave.
212-986-9400

Mann, David H.
666 Third Ave.
212-867-2720

Margeotes/Fertitta & Weiss, Inc.
130 Fifth Ave.
212-620-3838

Markland Corp.
1414 Ave. of the Americas
212-759-5440

Marks, Howard Advertising
655 Madison Ave.
212-752-7455

The Marschalk Co., Inc.
1345 Ave. of the Americas
212-408-8800

Marsteller, Inc.
866 Third Ave.
212-752-6500

McAdams, William Douglas
110 E. 59th St.
212-759-6300

McCaffrey and McCall
575 Lexington Ave.
212-421-7500

McCann/Erickson, Inc.
485 Lexington Ave.
212-697-6000

Medicus Intercon International,
    Inc.
909 Third Ave.
212-826-0760

Merling Marx & Seidman, Inc.
271 Madison Ave.
212-683-2100

Merritt, Stan, Advertising
369 Lexington Ave.
212-867-4650

Middle East Adv. & Mktg.
   Corp.
777 Third Ave.
212-838-7800

Millennium Design Comm. Inc.
350 Madison Ave.
212-986-4540

Miller Adv. Agency, Inc.
71 Fifth Ave.
212-929-2200

Mingo Jones Adv.
485 Lexington Ave.
212-697-4515

Moss & Company, Inc.
49 W. 38th St.
212-696-4110

Muir Cornelius Moore, Inc.
750 Third Ave.
212-687-4055

Muller Jordan Weiss
666 Fifth Ave.
212-399-2700

Nadler & Larimer, Inc.
1350 Ave. of the Americas
212-245-7300

Needham & Grohmann, Inc.
30 Rockefeller Plz.
212-245-6200

Newmark, Posner & Mitchell
300 E. 42nd St.
212-867-3900

Ogilvy & Mather Direct, Inc.
675 Third Ave.
212-986-6900

Ogilvy & Mather, Inc.
2 E. 48th St.
212-907-3400

Ogilvy & Mather Merchandising
2 E. 48th St.
212-688-6100

Ogilvy & Mather Partners, Inc.
380 Madison Ave.
212-687-2510

Ohlmeyer Adv.
9 W. 57th St.
212-872-9800

Pace Adv. Agency, Inc.
260 Madison Ave.
212-532-3550

Park Place Group, Inc.
157 E. 57th St.
212-838-6024

Parkson Adv. Agency, Inc.
767 Fifth Ave.
212-752-3300

Penchina Selkowitz Inc.
875 Third Ave.
212-980-6677

Peson, Sydney & Bernard Adv.
509 Madison Ave.
212-752-2212

Pfaff, Warren, Inc.
185 Madison Ave.
212-684-5550

Plapler & Associates Inc.
80 Fifth Ave.
212-807-7999

Popofsky Adv., Inc.
350 Fifth Ave.
212-279-5454

Poppe Tyson
475 Park Ave. S.
212-725-2900

Prendergast & Assoc., J. W.,
    Inc.
342 Madison Ave.
212-697-2720

Proclinica, Inc.
488 Madison Ave.
212-935-6440

R. C. Communications, Inc.
385 Madison Ave.
212-421-4500

R.S.M. & K., Inc.
770 Lexington Ave.
212-759-7070

Rapps & Collins, Inc.
475 Park Ave. S.
212-725-8100

Richard & Edwards, Inc.
750 Third Ave.
212-557-1600

Richmond Adv./Reinhold
    Assoc., Inc.
21 W. 38th St.
212-840-7676

Rogers, Peter & Assoc.
355 Lexington Ave.
212-599-0055

Romann & Tannenholz Adv.,
    Inc.
420 Lexington Ave.
212-755-5335

Rosenfeld Sirowitz Lawson, Inc.
111 Fifth Ave.
212-505-0200

Rosenthal, Albert Jay & Co.
545 Madison Ave.
212-826-6610

Rosenthal, Rolf Werner, Inc.
41 Madison Ave.
212-673-9330

Ruder & Finn, Inc.
110 E. 59th St.
212-593-6400

Rundle, J. B.
15 E. 26th St.
212-689-3070

Ruvane Leverte
6 E. 43rd St.
212-867-1670

SAMS, Inc.
475 Park Ave. S.
212-684-4242

SSC & B, Inc.
1 Dag Hammarskjold Plz.
212-605-8000

SZF, Inc.
104 Fifth Ave.
212-675-9071

Saas Advertising, Inc.
115 E. 57th St.
212-935-1141

Sacks & Rosen, Inc.
733 Third Ave.
212-986-4004

Salit, Murray & Assoc., Inc.
200 Park Ave.
212-661-7300

Sawdon & Bess, Inc.
444 Madison Ave.
212-751-6660

Saxton Communications Group,
   Ltd.
605 Third Ave.
212-953-1300

Scali, McCabe, Sloves, Inc.
800 Third Ave.
212-421-2050

Schein/Blattstein Adv., Inc.
420 Madison Ave.
212-758-1555

Schoenfeld/Straus
386 Park Ave. S.
212-889-1200

Scott, Louis
132 E. 35th St.
212-674-0215

Serino, Coyne & Nappi
1515 Broadway
212-869-9824

Shaller Rubin & Winer, Inc.
122 E. 25th St.
212-598-6900

Shapiro/Budrow & Assoc.
249 E. 32nd St.
212-532-9050

Shaw & Koulermos, Inc.
110 E. 59th St.
212-688-5290

Shaw & Todd, Inc.
6101 Empire State Bldg.
212-244-5225

Sheldon Fredericks Adv., Inc.
71 Vanderbilt Ave.
212-867-0110

Sherwood & Schneider, Inc.
625 Madison Ave.
212-486-8800

Siebel Mohr, Inc.
641 Lexington Ave.
212-593-0500

Slater, Hanft, Martin, Inc.
111 Fifth Ave.
212-674-3100

Smith/Greenland, Inc.
1414 Ave. of the Americas
212-752-5500

Smolen, Smith & Connolly
551 Fifth Ave.
212-687-7993

Soskin/Thompson
420 Lexington Ave.
212-210-8440

Specht/Gilbert & Partners, Inc.
445 Park Ave.
212-371-0590

Spier, Franklin, Inc.
270 Madison Ave.
212-679-4441

St. Vincent/Milone &
    McConnells Adv.
212-921-1414

Stogel, Philip
489 Fifth Ave.
212-682-7600

Stone & Adler Inc.
2 Park Ave.
212-578-4300

Sudler & Hennessey, Inc.
1633 Broadway
212-265-8000

Sudler & Hennessey, Inc.
1180 6th Ave.
212-869-2121

Sullivan & Brugnotelli
300 E. 42nd St.
212-986-4200

Sutton Communications
310 Madison Ave.
212-682-7090

Symon Hilliard, Inc.
48 E. 21 St.
212-505-0688

TBWA Advertising, Inc.
292 Madison Ave.
212-725-1150

TLK Direct Marketing
605 Third Ave.
212-972-9000

Tatham-Laird & L.
605 Third Ave.
212-972-9000

Telephone Marketing Programs,
    Inc.
1633 Broadway
212-977-4200

Thompson, J. Walter
466 Lexington Ave.
212-210-7000

Thompson-Koch Co., The, Inc.
90 Park Ave.
212-907-2369

193

Towne Silverstein Rotter
101 Park Ave.
212-557-5570

Treco Advertising, Inc.
205 E. 42nd St.
212-661-5140

Tromson Monroe Adv., Inc.
40 E. 49th St.
212-752-8660

Trout & Ries Advertising
1370 Ave. of Americas
212-869-8888

UniWorld Group, Inc.
1250 Broadway
212-564-0066

V & R Advertising, Inc.
919 Third Ave.
212-371-6040

Van Brunt & Co., Inc.
300 E. 42nd St.
212-949-1300

Venet Advertising, Inc.
888 Seventh Ave.
212-489-6700

Ventura Associates, Inc.
200 Madison Ave.
212-889-0707

Viola, Harry Adv.
650 Fifth Ave.
212-408-0428

Waring & LaRosa, Inc.
555 Madison Ave.
212-755-0700

Warner, Bicking & Fenwick, Inc.
866 United Nations Plz.
212-759-7900

Warren Kremer Adv., Inc.
2 Park Ave.
212-868-2914

Warren, Muller, Dolobowsky
747 Third Ave.
212-754-1600

Warwick Advertising
875 Third Ave.
212-751-4700

Weinstein, S. J. & Assoc.
100 Fifth Ave.
212-206-0222

Weiss & Geller, Inc.
880 Third Ave.
212-421-0600

Weiss, Michael B. Adv., Inc.
261 Madison Ave.
212-286-9300

Wellington Advertising, Inc.
271 Madison Ave.
212-683-7447

Wells, Rich, Greene, Inc.
767 Fifth Ave.
212-758-4300

Wilson, Edwin Bird, Inc.
136 Madison Ave.
212-684-5220

Winner Comms., Inc.
37 Union Square W.
212-421-8715

Wunderman Ricotta & Kline
575 Madison Ave.
212-909-0100

Wyse Advertising, Inc.
505 Park Ave.
212-752-9880

Young & Rubicam Intl, Inc.
285 Madison Ave.
212-210-3000

Young & Rubicam Special Market Div.
100 Park Ave.
212-210-5489

SAN FRANCISCO

Allen & Dorward, Inc.
747 Front St.
415-956-7470

Anderson/Miller Communications
846 California St.
415-986-1739

Arnold/Maxwell/Jackson & Smyth
440 Pacific Ave.
415-391-8425

BBDO/West
825 Battery St.
415-397-0346

Bruster/Archer/Ball
288 Seventh St.
415-861-0360

Busse & Cummins, Inc.
690 Fifth St.
415-957-0300

Campbell-Ewald Co.
201 California St.
415-989-5556

Chiat/Day, Inc.
414 Jackson Sq.
415-445-3000

Cunningham & Walsh, Inc.
500 Sansome St.
415-981-7850

DDB Needham
530 Bush St.
415-398-2669

DFS Dorland
415-982-8400

Dailey & Assoc.
574 Pacific Ave.
415-981-2250

D'Arcy Masius Benton &
    Bowles, Inc.
433 California St.
415-391-2750

Davis Johnson Mogul Colom-
    batto
27 Maiden Ln.
415-421-9970

Doremus & Co.
690 Market St.
415-981-4020

Evans, San Francisco, Inc.
535 Pacific Ave.
415-986-6178

Foote, Cone & Belding/Honig
1255 Battery St.
415-398-5200

Gardner Communications, Inc.
27 Maiden Ln.
415-434-2191

Goodby, Berlin & Silverstein
66 Broadway
415-392-0669

Grey Advertising, Inc.
50 California St.
415-362-0393

Harrison Assoc., Claire
54 Mint St.
415-543-7760

Ketchum Advertising
55 Union St.
415-781-9480

Lowey & Partners, Inc.
921 Front St.
415-392-3010

Lynch & Rockey Adv.
680 Beach St.
415-441-6485

McCann Erickson, Inc.
201 California St.
415-981-2262

Michael/Sellers Adv.
760 Market St.
415-781-7200

Ogilvy & Mather, Inc.
735 Battery St.
415-981-0950

Pinne, Garvin & Hock, Inc.
200 Vallejo St.
415-956-4210

Public Media Center
25 Scotland St.
415-434-1403

Rainoldi-Bowles, Inc.
The Hearst Bldg.
415-974-1830

Scroggin & Fischer Advertising
843 Montgomery St.
415-391-2694

Soskin/Thompson Assoc.
4 Embarcadero Center
415-955-2000

Thompson, J. Walter
4 Embarcadero Center
415-955-2000

Vicom Associates
901 Battery St.
415-391-8700

Wilton, Coombs & Colnett,
    Inc., Advertising
855 Front St.
415-981-6250

Wodell, Jack
582 Market St.
415-391-1350

TORONTO

Adventure Advertising Int'l
10 Mary St.
416-968-7550

Ambrose Carr De Forest &
    Linton, Ltd.
110 Laird Dr.
416-425-8200

Baker Lovick Ltd.
60 Bloor St. W.
416-924-6861

Base Brown & Partners, Ltd.
512 King St. E.
416-364-5044

Bates, Ted Advertising, Inc.
790 Bay St.
416-597-1616

Borg Advertising Ltd.
185 Bloor St. E.
416-923-1146

Bozell Jacobs Kenyon &
    Eckhardt
70 The Esplanade
416-364-3400

Burnett, Leo
165 University Ave.
416-366-5801

Burson/Marsteller Public Rela-
    tions
80 Bloor St. W.
416-964-8300

Camp Associates Advertising,
    Ltd.
1910 Yonge St.
416-484-6000

Carder Gray Advertising, Inc.
22 St. Clair Ave. E.
416-925-2285

Cardon Rose, Inc.
112 St. Clair Ave. W.
416-924-7361

Case Associates Adv. Ltd.
2300 Yonge St.
416-481-4281

Cockfield Brown Inc.
1 St. Clair Ave. E.
416-964-9000

Crombie Advertising Co., Ltd.
481 University Ave.
416-368-7031

DDB Needham
2 Bloor St. W.
416-925-8911

D'Arcy Masius Benton &
      Bowles Canada, Ltd.
1235 Bay St.
416-922-2221

Enterprise Adv. Assocs., Ltd.
1075 Bay St.
416-967-1444

Foote, Cone & Belding Adv.
496 Queen St. E.
416-365-7111

Foster Advertising, Ltd.
40 Clair Ave. W.
416-928-8000

Gloucester Group, The
415 Yonge St.
416-977-8972

Goodis-Wolf, Inc.
130 Adelaide St. W.
416-863-0500

Grant Tandy Advertising
365 Bloor St. E.
416-968-0201

Gray O'Rourke Sussman, Inc.
120 Eglinton Ave. E.
416-485-7400

Grey Advertising, Ltd.
1075 Bay St.
416-967-0600

Hartford, D.W. & Assoc., Inc.
80 Gerrard St. E.
416-977-8889

Hayhurst Advertising, Ltd.
55 Eglinton Ave. E.
416-487-4371

Hill, Gordon Adv. Ltd.
130 Bloor St. W.
416-924-8481

Ian Roberts Inc.
3080 Yonge St.
416-484-0111

JWT Direct
102 Bloor St. W.
416-924-2574

Kelley, Russell T., Inc.
920 Yonge St.
416-967-7895

Kert Advertising, Ltd.
2200 Yonge St.
416-481-6422

Lee, Raymond & Assoc.
401 Wellington St. W.
416-596-6400

MacLaren Advertising Co., Ltd.
415 Yonge St.
416-977-2244

Marshall Fenn, Ltd.
245 Davenport Rd.
416-962-3241

McCann-Erickson
151 Bloor St. W.
416-925-3231

McCann-Erickson, Adv. of
    Canada
830 W. Pender, Vancouver
604-689-1131

Mc Kim Advertising, Ltd.
Commerce Ct. E.
416-863-5300

McLauchlan, Mohr, Massey,
    Ltd.
77 River St.
416-367-1430

Media Advertising, Ltd.
180 Bloor St. W.
416-922-0700

Price, Rubin & Partners, Inc.
105 Carlton St.
416-591-1200

SMW Advertising, Ltd.
240 Eglinton Ave.
416-486-7411

SSC&B Lintas
48 St. Clair Ave. W.
416-961-6322

Scali, McCabe, Sloves, Ltd.
2 St. Clair Ave. E.
416-961-3817

Thompson, J. Walter Co. Ltd.
102 Bloor St. W.
416-920-9171

Young & Rubicam, Ltd.
60 Bloor St. W.
416-961-5111